Catrin E. Morris

# FLASH
## on English
## for TOURISM

# Contents

🎧 1  MP3 audio files downloadable from www.elionline.com

3

# 1 | An Introduction to Travel and Tourism

**1** **Look at the pictures and answer the questions.**

1 Do these people travel?
2 Are they tourists?

**2** Read the text about travel and tourism and check your answers.

People travel for lots of reasons. They make journeys to and from school or work every day; visit friends and family; take day trips shopping or to football matches; go out for evening entertainment such as the cinema; and they go away on business or study trips. So when does travel become tourism? When people travel to and stay in a place which is not where they live. For example there is recreational tourism if you want to relax and have fun, maybe at the beach. There's cultural tourism: sightseeing or visiting museums to learn about history, art and people's lifestyles. With adventure tourism you explore distant places or do extreme activities. Ecotourism is about ethical and responsible trips to natural environments such as rainforests. Winter tourism is usually holidays in resorts where there is snow and people go skiing or snowboarding. Sport tourism is to play or watch different sporting events like the Olympics. Educational tourism is to learn something, possibly a foreign language, abroad. Nowadays there is also health tourism to look after your body and mind by visiting places like spa resorts; religious tourism to celebrate religious events or visit important religious places such as Mecca for Muslims; and gap-year tourism when young people go backpacking or do voluntary work between school and university.

**3** Read the text again. Match the type of tourism with its definition and an example.

| Type of tourism | Definition | Example |
|---|---|---|
| Adventure tourism | holidays to resorts where there is snow | a foreign language |
| Cultural tourism | to celebrate religious event or visit important religious places | any of the other kinds of tourism |
| Ecotourism | to explore distant places or do extreme activities | Mecca for Muslims |
| Educational tourism | to learn about history, art and people's lifestyles | monuments or museums |
| Gap year tourism | to learn something | rainforests |
| Health tourism | to look after your body and mind | skiing or snowboarding |
| Recreational tourism | to play or watch different sporting events | spa resorts |
| Religious tourism | to take ethical and responsible trips to natural environments | the beach |
| Sport tourism | to relax and have fun | the Olympics Games |
| Winter tourism | when young people go backpacking or do voluntary work between school and university | trekking |

**4** Read the text again and underline the correct answer to each question.

1 People travel
   A for different reasons.      B to go on holiday.      C to get to work.
2 You can take
   A day and evening trips.      B study and business trips.      C theatre and cinema trips.
3 Tourism is travel
   A in your home town.      B to countries across the world.      C to places where you don't live.
4 Ecotourism is ethical and responsible about
   A money.      B shopping.      C the environment.
5 The Olympics is a
   A sporting event.      B summer event.      C winter event.
6 A spa is a place you visit to
   A celebrate a religious event.      B learn something new.      C look after your health.

**5** 🎧 1 Listen to a conversation about where to go on holiday and match each member of the family with the type of tourism they would like from exercise 3.

1 Dad *cultural*                        4 Josh _____
2 Grandma _____          5 Mum _____
3 Hannah _____           6 Zoe _____

**6** 🎧 2 Complete the conversation below between a travel agent and a customer with expressions from the box. Listen and check your answers.

| Any ideas   How about   I agree   I quite fancy   I really want to   Let's see   Personally, I'd like   Why don't you |

Travel Agent:   (1) *Any ideas* about where you want to go on holiday this summer, Mrs Brown?
Customer:       Well, (2) _____ have a proper family holiday this year.
Travel Agent:   OK, there are some good all inclusive package holidays by the sea.
Customer:       Mmm! (3) _____ going somewhere different this year.
Travel Agent:   (4) _____ taking a city break?
Customer:       (5) _____ it, but I think the kids might be bored.
Travel Agent:   (6) _____ combine a city break with something for the kids like Euro Disney?
Customer:       That's a good idea, (7) _____, but isn't Euro Disney really expensive?
Travel Agent:   Well, (8) _____ if there are any special offers on at the moment.

**7** Work in pairs: A and B. Look at the pictures in exercise 1 of different holiday destinations and role play a conversation between a travel agent and a customer. Try to use expressions from exercise 6.

Student A: you are a travel agent. Ask questions about what kind of holiday the customer wants this year.
Student B: you are a customer. Answer questions about what kind of holiday you want this year. When you finish, change roles.

**8** Read the text and complete the table with the correct information.

Tourism is a multi-billion dollar business with hundreds of millions of travellers arriving in destinations across the world every year, but there's a lot more to tourism than just the tourists.

Before you even leave home you probably use a number of services. You book your trip through a tour operator, if it's a package holiday, or a travel agent, if you want to buy products and services like flights separately. These days, many people book directly online with companies that offer both organised and independent travel. You usually need to purchase airline, train, ferry and coach tickets to your holiday resort in advance to reserve a seat and get a good price. If you're hiring a car it's also a good idea to book in advance, but you can arrange local transport like taxis and buses when you're there. You also need to book accommodation to be sure to stay where you want, when you want. There is a wide range of options for different people and pockets: from luxury hotels to roadside motels, family-run guesthouses or B&Bs (Bed and Breakfasts), to self-catering apartments to youth hostels. You can decide about hospitality (catering and entertainment) during your holiday, unless you book it with your accommodation. B&B means you get breakfast included in the price of your stay. Half board, usually only available at hotels, means breakfast and dinner are included. Full board means breakfast, lunch and dinner are included. This option is common on package or cruise ship holidays to keep the cost down, as are all inclusive leisure activities such as sport, shopping and live shows. Most places have a Tourist Information Point where they give you free information about what to see and do and how to get around. Organised trips often have travel reps (representatives) on hand to help you, but you can also pay a local tour guide to take you sightseeing or show you tourist attractions.

| Hospitality | | | | | |
|---|---|---|---|---|---|
| **Accommodation** (Where to stay) | **Catering** (Where to eat) | **Entertainment and leisure** (What to do) | **Jobs** (Who does what) | **Transport** (How to travel) | **Holiday types** (What kind of holiday) |
| luxury hotels | bed and breakfast | sport | tour operator | plane | package holiday |

**9** Read the text again and answer the questions.

1 How many travellers arrive in destinations across the world every year?
2 How can you book holidays?
3 Why do you need to purchase tickets for airlines, trains, ferries and coaches in advance?
4 What other transport service is it a good idea to book in advance?
5 When can you arrange local transport?
6 For whom and what is there a wide range of different accommodation options?
7 Which kind of accommodation includes breakfast, lunch and dinner?
8 Where is this a common option?
9 Do you pay for information from Tourist Information Points?
10 Who can take you sightseeing or show you tourist attractions?

**10** Complete the online travel search information.

## Holidays you like
Trip Search...

HOLIDAY TYPE (only tick [✓] one)
Package holiday ☐            Transport & accommodation ☐
Transport only ☐             Accommodation only ☐            Transport, accommodation and car hire ☐

TRANSPORT (tick one or more)
Flight ☐
Car hire ☐                                              Ferry tickets ☐
Train tickets ☐                                         Coach tickets ☐
Leaving from:_____ Departure date:_____ Time:_____ Going to:_____ Return date:_____ Time:_____

Accommodation (only tick one)                    Catering (only tick one)
Hotel ☐       B&B ☐            Full board ☐              Breakfast only ☐
Motel ☐       Apartment ☐      Half board ☐              Self-catering ☐
Guesthouse ☐  Youth hostel ☐

Entertainment & leisure interests (you can tick more than one)
Adventure ☐    extreme sport ☐   trekking ☐
Culture ☐      museums ☐         art galleries ☐   sightseeing ☐
Ecotourism ☐   natural world ☐   conservation ☐
Educational ☐  arts & crafts ☐   cooking ☐         languages ☐   music & drama ☐
Gap year ☐     backpacking ☐     voluntary work ☐
Health ☐       spa resorts ☐     yoga & meditation ☐
Religious ☐    events ☐          places ☐
Recreational ☐ seaside ☐         shopping ☐        shows ☐
Sport ☐        playing ☐         watching ☐
                                 which sport(s): _____

**11** There is a problem with the *Holidays you like* online booking system. Write them an email giving them the information in your trip search. Use these expressions to help you.

| | | |
|---|---|---|
| I want to book... | I want to leave on... at... | I'm interested in... tourism |
| I'd like to travel by... | I'd like to return on... at... | In particular, I'd like to... |
| I'm leaving from... | I'd like to book accommodation in | |
| I'm going to... | a... with (catering) | |

## MY GLOSSARY

accommodation /əkɒməˈdeɪʃn/ _____
airline /ˈeəlaɪn/ _____
backpacking /ˈbækpækɪŋ/_____
to book /tə bʊk/ _____
catering /ˈkeɪtərɪŋ/ _____
cruise /kruːz/ _____
entertainment /entəˈteɪnmənt/ _____
guesthouse /ˈgesthaʊs/_____
flight /flaɪt/ _____
full board /fʊl bɔːd/ _____
half board /hɑːf bɔːd/ _____
to hire /tə haɪr/ _____
hospitality /hɒspɪˈtæləti/_____
journey /ˈdʒɜːni/ _____
leisure /ˈleʒə(r)/ _____
luxury hotel /ˈlʌkʃri həʊˈtel/ _____

package holiday /ˈpækɪdʒ ˈhɒlɪdeɪ/_____
to purchase /tə ˈpɜːtʃəs/ _____
recreational /rekriˈeɪʃənəl/ _____
to reserve /tə rɪˈzɜːv/_____
roadside motel /ˈrəʊdsaɪd məʊˈtel/ _____
self-catering /selfˈkeɪtərɪŋ/ _____
sightseeing /ˈsaɪtsiːɪŋ/ _____
spa resort /spɑː rɪˈzɔːt/ _____
to take a break /tə teɪk ə breɪk/ _____
tour guide /tʊə(r) gaɪd/_____
tour operator /tʊə(r) pəreɪtə(r)/ _____
travel representative /trævl reprɪˈzentətɪv/ _____
tourist information point /ˈtʊərɪst ɪnfəˈmeɪʃn pɔɪnt/ ____
travel agent /trævl ˈeɪdʒnt/_____
youth hostel /juːθ ˈhɒstl/ _____

# 2 | Tourism Organisations, Promotion and Marketing

**1** **Look at these company logos and answer the questions.**

1  Do you recognise these company logos?
2  What type of companies are they?

A   B   C

**2** **Read the text about tourism organisations and check your answers.**

Tourism organisations fall into three categories. Firstly they can be non-governmental organisations or a charity like the World Tourism Organisation, a United Nations' organisation which promotes 'the development of responsible, sustainable and universally accessible tourism' (UNWTO). Secondly, they can be government organisations like Britain's national tourism agency, Visit Britain, which markets British tourism at home and abroad. Thirdly, they can be private sector organisations like Thomas Cook, which promote and sell holidays for profit.

We can separate this last group into three more categories. Independent companies have one or more branches, which can often be close to each other. They sell their holidays to people locally and market them by word of mouth. Miniple companies have several branches in different areas, which sometimes use different trade names and they have a head office, which can manage the organisation's marketing strategy centrally. Multiple agencies have branches in all major towns and cities and they can be part of very large tourism sector companies. They market holidays on the basis of competitive prices or special offer packages. In addition to this, travel agents can be members of trade associations, organisations representing travel companies who can help with marketing and protect customers' rights. Of course nowadays many people prefer online do-it-yourself tourism to any of these organisations.

**3** **Read the text again and complete the table.**

| Category of tourism organisation | Example | Type of organisation and what they do |
|---|---|---|
| non-governmental organisations/ a charity | UNWTO | |
| | | markets British tourism at home and abroad |
| private sector organisations | | |
| independent | | have one or more branches, ... |
| miniple | | |
| multiple | | |
| trade associations | | |

**4** **Write the equivalent word in your language.**

1 charity: _____
2 sustainable: _____
3 to promote: _____
4 profit: _____
5 branch: _____

6 to market: _____
7 word of mouth: _____
8 trade name: _____
9 head office: _____
10 competitive: _____

**5** 🎧 3 **Complete this text about the National Trust with the words and expressions in exercise 4. Be careful to use the appropriate grammatical form. Then listen and check.**

The National Trust is a (1) *charity* and a non-(2) _____ organisation, which (3) _____ British tourism to artistic, historical and natural sites in a (4) _____ way. It has two (5) _____, one in London and another in Swindon, as well as hundreds of (6) _____ all over the UK. Places with the (7) _____, 'National Trust' (8) _____ themselves through the image of conservation and heritage. However, many of the thousands of visitors to National Trust sites hear about them by (9) _____ from friends, colleagues or relatives. They provide great days out for the whole family as you can enter many sites for free and you can also hire venues for special events at extremely (10) _____ prices.

**Dunster Castle, Somerset**

**6** **Read the short descriptions of National Trust sites and match a person with a place to visit.**

🌳 **National Trust**

1 **Wellbrook Beetling Mill:** do you like trying new crafts? Do you enjoy going for walks in the country and having picnics on the lawn? Then come to this water-powered linen mill in Northern Ireland. It's open 2-6 p.m. March to September.
2 **South Foreland Lighthouse:** can you imagine living and working in a lighthouse on the White Cliffs of Dover overlooking the sea, at the time of the first international radio transmission? Find out what it's like and learn about Marconi and Faraday's early experiments, March to October, 11 a.m. to 5.30 p.m.
3 **Red house, Kent:** if you love looking at beautiful things, this is the place for you. You can see William Morris's art nouveau furniture, Edward Burne-Jones's original artwork, or try relaxing and playing games in the landscaped garden. Open March to December 11 a.m. to 5 p.m.
4 **Theatre Royal, Suffolk:** do you have a passion for drama? Visit Britain's last Regency theatre. You can see the amazing hand-painted ceiling. It's just like the sky! Then watch a 19th-century-style play. Open February to November, Tuesday and Thursday p.m., Saturday and Sunday a.m. Entrance is free. You only pay for performances.
5 **Dunster Castle, Somerset:** are you mad about history? Explore the secret passage in the medieval castle. Discover the Lovers' Bridge in the gardens. Go bat-watching in the great hall. Find out about the lives of Dunster's noble families. Visit the gardens all year round, 11-4 in winter, 11-5 in summer. The castle opens March to October 11-5.

a ☐ *1* Claudia is quite artistic and she loves trying new things. She doesn't like science, but she likes being in the country.
b ☐ David likes art and architecture and he also enjoys relaxing and playing games. He hates learning about history.
c ☐ Gwen is mad about history and drama. She hates being outside and doesn't really like gardens or nature.
d ☐ Holli is very romantic and likes investigating mysteries and nature-watching. She's also quite interested in history and gardening.
e ☐ Mick has a passion for science and loves finding out about how things work. He doesn't like going to museums or to theatres.

**7** **Work in pairs. Follow the instructions below, then swap roles.**

Student A: Ask your partner about their interests. Then choose the best activity for them from exercise 6.

Student B: Tell your partner about your interests and what you like and don't like doing. Do you agree with Student A's choice of activity for you?

**8** **Match the terms with the correct definitions.**

1 Advertising      a ☐ It keeps a product or service in the minds of customers and helps stimulate their demand for it.

2 Promotion      b ☐ It makes sure that customers buy a product or service by understanding and meeting their needs.

3 Marketing      c ☐ It brings a product or service to the attention of customers through the media to persuade them to buy it.

**9** **Read the text and check your answers.**

People are often unclear about exactly what marketing is, and confuse it with advertising and promotion, both important parts of marketing. Advertising brings a product or service to the attention of customers through the media e.g. newspapers, TV, or the Internet to persuade them to buy it. Promotion keeps a product or service in the minds of customers and helps stimulate their demand for it, often through advertising. Marketing is altogether more complex. It is all the activities involved in making sure that customers buy a product or service by understanding and meeting their needs. Traditionally this is called the four Ps marketing mix: Product; Price; Place; Promotion. In other words you need to market the right product at the right price in the right place and in the right way if you want to sell it. You could add one other P to this: you need to sell it to the right people.

You can identify the right people through a process called market segmentation. This is when you group together people with similar needs and wants to identify your target customers so you can successfully market your product to them. There are many ways of doing this, for instance: by the amount of money people have (do they want budget or luxury holidays?); by the kind of activities they're interested in (heritage, nature or adventure); by their circumstances (are they single, a couple, or a family?); by their age (18-25 or 60+); and by the kind of tourists they are (independent or pampered).

**10** **Read the text again quickly and answer the questions.**

1 Give three examples of advertising media. *Newspapers, TV and the Internet*

2 Give an example of Promotion.

3 Name the four Ps of the Marketing mix.

4 Name the fifth P.

5 Name the process of grouping together people with similar needs and wants in marketing.

6 Give three examples of this.

**11** 🎧 4 **Listen to the interview with a travel agent about his company's e-marketing strategies and decide if these sentences are true (T) or false (F). Correct the false ones.**

1 They use TV and radio adverts. *F*
   *No, they don't use them because they are too expensive.*

2 They sometimes place ads in newspapers or magazines they think their target customers buy.

3 They advertise in specialist travel brochures, leaflets or tourism guides.

4 Their main marketing area is online.

5 They use a combination of low-cost e-marketing strategies.

6 They don't like social networking sites.

7 They never advertise on search engines.

8 Banners are not competitive and they don't always reach the target customers.

9 It's not possible to book online.

10 They have great word of mouth marketing through their forum.

**12** Work in pairs. Look at the list of different kinds of media advertising and discuss which you think you could use to market holidays for each group.

> newspapers   TV   the Internet   radio   magazines   travel brochures   leaflets   tourism guides
> social networking sites   search engine banners   websites   online forum   word of mouth

1  A big family who want an all inclusive package holiday
2  A retired couple interested in history and heritage
3  A group of friends who want an adventure holiday
4  A young married couple
5  A gap-year student
6  A young person looking for a cheap city break
7  A group of friends looking for a last minute offer
8  You!

Student A: *I think we could use newspapers or tourism brochures to market an all inclusive package holiday to a big family.*
Student B: *I don't agree. I think everybody uses the Internet these days, so maybe we could use a search engine banner or a website.*

**13** Work in groups of three. Look at the picture of a holiday destination. You are the marketing team for a big travel company. Choose your target customer and write an advert marketing the holiday to them. Remember the 4 Ps (Product, Place, Price and Promotion) and decide what media to advertise through. In your advert, include details of:

• suitable activities for customers to do
• facilities and services you offer
• the price (with offers/discounts)
• the length and period of the holiday (try to suit it to your customers)
• other information to attract your customers

## MY GLOSSARY

ad\advert\advertisement /æd/ /ˈædvɜːt/ /ədˈvɜːtɪsmənt/ __
to advertise /tuː ˈædvətaɪz/ _____
artwork /ˈɑːtwɜːk/ _____
banner /ˈbænə(r)/ _____
budget /ˈbʌdʒɪt/ _____
craft /krɑːft/_____
customers' rights /ˈkʌstəmərz raɪts/_____
demand /dɪˈmɑːnd/ _____
development /dɪˈveləpmənt/_____
DIY (do-it-yourself) /duː ɪt jɔːˈself/_____
e-marketing /iːˈmɑːkɪtɪŋ/_____
government organisation /ˈgʌvənmənt ɔːgnəˈzeɪʃn/____
heritage /ˈherɪtɪdʒ/_____
landscaped garden /ˈlændskeɪpd ˈgɑːdən/ _____
lawn /lɔːn/_____
leaflet /ˈliːflət/ _____

locally /ˈləʊkli/_____
market segmentation /ˈmɑːkɪt segmenˈteɪʃn/_____
marketing tool /ˈmɑːkɪtɪŋ tuːl/_____
to meet the needs /tə miːt ðə niːdz/_____
mill /mɪl/ _____
miniple /ˈmɪnɪpl/ _____
multiple /ˈmʌltɪpl/ _____
(non-)governmental organisation /nɒngʌvənmənt ɔː gnəˈzeɪʃn/_____
pampered /ˈpæmpə(r)d/ _____
to protect /tə prəˈtekt/_____
search engine /sɜːtʃ ˈendʒɪn/_____
to stimulate /tə ˈstɪmjʊleɪt/ _____
target customers /ˈtɑːgɪt ˈkʌstəmə(r)z/ _____
trade association /treɪd əsəʊsiˈeɪʃn/ _____
trade name /treɪd neɪm/_____

# 3 Types of Transport

**1** Read the four texts about different types of transport and match them with the pictures.

**1** [ ] Air travel is a fast way of travelling both for domestic and international journeys. Some airline companies operate scheduled flights, when take-off and landing are at major airports in major cities. Because departure and arrival times are regular and guaranteed tickets can be expensive. Alternatively, there are cheap charter flights when a travel company buys all the seats on a plane and sells at a discounted price. Charter airlines and low-cost scheduled airlines often operate from more accessible local airports and fly direct to holiday resorts, particularly in peak season. You usually need to buy tickets in advance. It is also possible to buy round the world tickets where you stop off at different global destinations. There is a limit to how much luggage passengers can carry and it takes time to check-in for flights due to security checks. Nowadays many people try to avoid taking too many flights because they aren't good for the environment.

**2** [ ] Sea travel can be a clean alternative to air travel. Ferries operate from one mainland destination to another, or between islands, departing and arriving at major ports. You can often take your car on ferries and there are no limits on the luggage you can carry. Journeys are long compared to flights and they can be quite expensive, especially if you sleep in a cabin overnight. You can buy tickets directly from the ferry companies or through tour operators, usually in advance. You can also take a luxury cruise, but they are generally quite expensive, all-inclusive packages.

**3** [ ] Rail travel also has a low environmental impact and is a very flexible and convenient mode of transport because you can buy tickets in advance or just turn up at the station. Price varies a lot according to distance and destination. Luggage allowance is limited on trains, but on long distance trips you can book a bed to sleep in, called a berth. There are also young person's rail passes for travelling around Europe and many countries have cheap or subsidised rail travel.

**4** [ ] Road travel can be by car or by coach, but neither is very environmentally friendly. Car travel is very convenient because you can choose your own departure and arrival points and times, and take as much luggage as your vehicle can carry. The cost is generally low apart from fuel and any tolls, but travel time can be long. Alternatively you can arrive at your destination and hire a car on arrival, but this can be expensive. Coaches, like trains, follow timetables and you need to buy tickets in advance to be sure of a seat. Journeys can be slow and arrival times are unpredictable because of traffic. They are however cheap and convenient, with stops at both major and minor destinations.

**2** Match these words and expressions from the text with their definitions.

1 charter flight     a [ ] a plane leaving at the same time each day or each week
2 environmentally friendly     b [ ] a plane journey organised by a company that buys all the seats
3 fuel     c [ ] a special train ticket you can buy to travel around a specific area for a specific period of time
4 landing
5 luggage     d [ ] bags and suitcases that you take on a journey
6 peak season     e [ ] something that doesn't damage the natural world
7 rail pass     f [ ] the activities to protect a country, building or person against attack or danger
8 scheduled flight     g [ ] the time of year when a lot of people go on holiday
9 security checks     h [ ] what we put in a car to make it go, e.g. petrol or diesel
10 take-off     i [ ] when an airplane leaves the ground and starts flying
    j [ ] when the plane returns to the ground at the end of a journey

**3** Read the four texts again and answer the questions. Be careful, some have more than one answer.

Which type of transport:
1 can be quite expensive if you travel overnight?
  *sea*
2 has a low environmental impact?
3 has a luxury version with all-inclusive packages?
4 has limits on passenger luggage?
5 has long security checks?
6 has unpredictable arrival times?
7 is convenient because you can choose your own route?
8 is not environmentally friendly?
9 operates between mainlands or islands?
10 has guaranteed departure and arrival times?

**4** 🎧 5 Listen to the conversation and decide where it takes place (in a ticket office, travel agency, tour operator's, on the phone) and what kind of tickets the customer wants to buy.

**5** 🎧 5 Listen to the conversation again and complete it with the missing information.

| | |
|---|---|
| Woman: | Hello, I'd like to buy a ticket to (1) *London* please. |
| Ticket officer: | Is that a (2) _____ or a (3) _____ ticket? |
| Woman: | A (4) _____ please. |
| Ticket officer: | When do you want to (5) _____? |
| Woman: | Now. |
| Ticket officer: | And when do you want to (6) _____? |
| Woman: | Today, please. (7) _____ is that? |
| Ticket officer: | A (8) _____ day return ticket is (9) _____. |
| Woman: | What time is the next (10) _____? |
| Ticket officer: | It's at (11) _____ from platform (12) _____. |
| Woman: | Thank you. |

**6** Work in pairs. Role play conversations at the ticket office. Use the dialogue from exercise 5 to help you. Then swap roles.

**7** Read these airport procedures and put them in the order you should do them. The first and the last are done for you.
a ☐1 Arrive at the airport and go to the correct check-in desk.
b ☐ Check in your luggage and take your boarding pass.
c ☐ Give the airline staff your passport and booking information.
d ☐ Present your boarding card and identification for inspection at passport control.
e ☐ Proceed to the departure gate when it opens.
f ☐ Put your hand luggage and coat through the security check.
g ☐8 Show your passport and boarding card to staff before boarding.
h ☐ Walk through the metal detector.

**8** 🎧 6 Now listen and check.

**9** Read the conversation below between an airline steward and a customer and complete it with the expressions from the box.

A window seat, please.   ~~Here they are.~~
Just one.   Yes, I did.
Good, it doesn't weigh very much.

| | |
|---|---|
| Airline steward: | Good morning, can I have your passport and booking information, please? |
| Customer: | (1) *Here they are.* |
| Airline steward: | Would you like a window or an aisle seat? |
| Customer: | (2) _____ |
| Airline steward: | Did you pack your bag yourself? |
| Customer: | (3) _____ |
| Airline steward: | Put your bag on the scales, please. |
| Customer: | (4) _____ |
| Airline steward: | How many pieces of hand luggage have you got? |
| Customer: | (5) _____ |
| Airline steward: | Here are your passport and boarding pass. You need to go to gate 3 at 14.20. |

# 3

**10** Match these transport symbols you see in airports with the words in the box.

> buses   car hire   parking   taxis   trains   underground

1 _____

2 _____

3 _____

4 _____

5 _____

6 _____

**11** Read the text and complete the table.

> You're at your holiday destination, and now you need to continue your journey. Taxis are quick and efficient for short journeys, but they can be expensive. Many charge per passenger, piece of luggage, as well as surcharges for airport and night time journeys. If you want to be free to travel when and where you like, car hire can offer good value. You pay a daily or weekly rate for hiring a car, plus fuel costs and you choose the kind of car you want, but most are bad for the environment. Adventurous tourists can rent a motorbike, moped or bicycle. These are cheaper and also more environmentally-friendly, but watch out for traffic or people stealing your bike! For people on a budget, public transport is a good and green option. Cities usually have a choice of underground, buses, trains and sometimes trams and cable cars too. In small towns, the options are more limited. Cost and convenience vary a lot in different places, so look out for special offers like combination tickets, weekend or all-day travel passes. Of course if you want to save your money and the planet, you could always walk!

| Mode of transport | Positive things about it | Negative things about it |
|---|---|---|
| taxi | | |
| | | bad for the environment |
| motorbike | adventurous | |
| public transport | good for people on a budget | cost and convenience vary a lot |

**12** Read the email below. Who is it to?

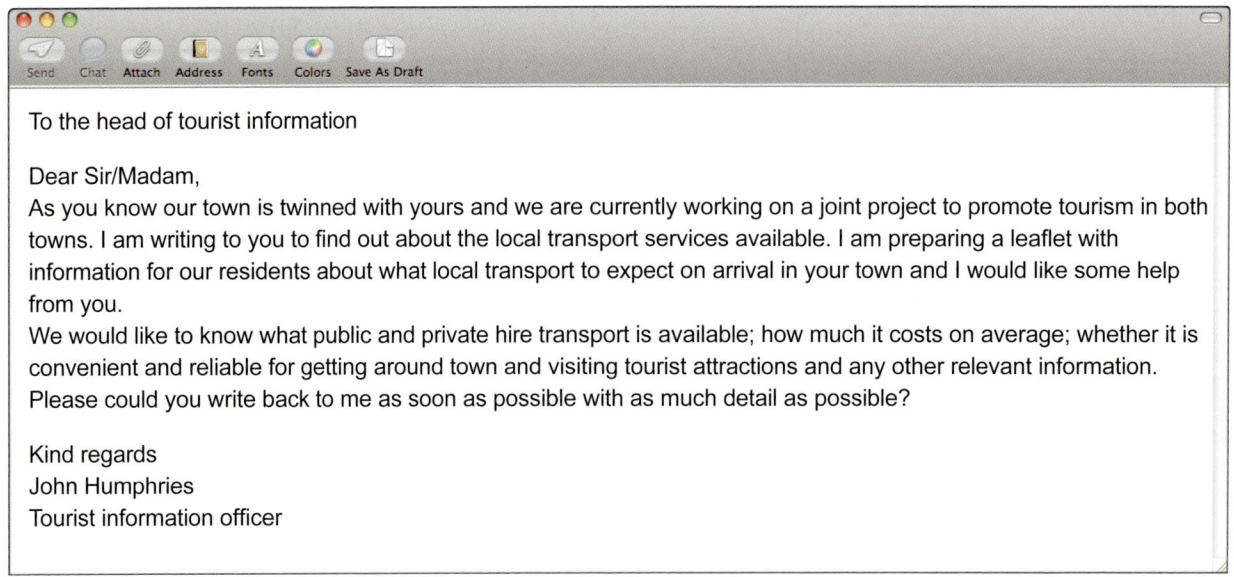

Send   Chat   Attach   Address   Fonts   Colors   Save As Draft

To the head of tourist information

Dear Sir/Madam,
As you know our town is twinned with yours and we are currently working on a joint project to promote tourism in both towns. I am writing to you to find out about the local transport services available. I am preparing a leaflet with information for our residents about what local transport to expect on arrival in your town and I would like some help from you.
We would like to know what public and private hire transport is available; how much it costs on average; whether it is convenient and reliable for getting around town and visiting tourist attractions and any other relevant information.
Please could you write back to me as soon as possible with as much detail as possible?

Kind regards
John Humphries
Tourist information officer

14

**13** Read the email again and answer the questions.

1  Who is the email from?
2  What is the relationship between the two towns?
3  What is the joint project for?

4  Why is John Humphries writing?
5  What information does he want to know?
6  When would he like to receive a reply?

**14** You work at a tourist information office. Your boss shows you Mr Humphries's email and asks you to complete this survey about transport available in your town.

| PUBLIC TRANSPORT | |
|---|---|
| [Please tick your answers] | |
| • What public transport is available? | ☐ underground ☐ buses ☐ trams ☐ trains ☐ cable cars ☐ other _____ |
| • Are they reliable services? | ☐ yes, usually ☐ not always ☐ sometimes ☐ not usually |
| • How much does an average journey cost? | _____ |
| • Are there a lot of stops around town? | ☐ Yes, there are. ☐ No, there aren't. |
| • Are they convenient for tourist attractions? | ☐ Yes, they are. ☐ Yes, some are. ☐ No, they aren't. |
| • Where can you buy tickets for public transport? | ☐ on board ☐ at the stop/station ☐ other _____ |
| • Are there any problems with these modes of transport? | ☐ traffic ☐ overcrowding ☐ crime ☐ other _____ |

**15** Write a reply to John Humphries's email, using the information in your transport survey. Be honest about the local transport available, but be as positive as possible. Remember you want tourists to visit your town!

*Dear Mr Humphries,*
*Thank you for your recent email. In answer to your questions...*

_____
_____
_____
_____

*Kind regards*

## MY GLOSSARY

airline steward /ˈeəlaɪn ˈstjuːəd/ _____
aisle seat /aɪl siːt/ _____
berth /bɜːθ/ _____
boarding pass /ˈbɔːdɪŋ pɑːs/ _____
cable car /ˈkeɪbl̩ kɑːr/ _____
to charge /tə tʃɑːdʒ/ _____
cheap day return /tʃiːp deɪ rɪˈtɜːn/ _____
coach /kəʊtʃ/ _____
departure /dɪˈpɑːtʃə(r)/ _____
discounted price /dɪˈskaʊntɪd praɪs/ _____
environmentally-friendly /ɪnvaɪərən'mentli frendli/ ____
ferry /ˈferi/ _____
fuel /fjʊəl/ _____
gate /geɪt/ _____
hand luggage /hænd ˈlʌgɪdʒ/ _____
landing /ˈlændɪŋ/ _____
long distance /lɒŋ ˈdɪstns/ _____
low environmental impact /ləʊ ɪnvaɪərən'mentl̩ ˈɪmpækt/_
luggage allowance /ˈlʌgɪdʒ əˈlaʊns/ _____
mainland /ˈmeɪnlænd/ _____

moped /ˈməʊped/ _____
motorbike /ˈməʊtəbaɪk/ _____
overcrowding /əʊvəˈkraʊdɪŋ/ _____
overnight /əʊvəˈnaɪt/ _____
passenger /ˈpæsəndʒə(r)/ _____
peak season /piːk ˈsiːzn/ _____
platform /ˈplætfɔːm/ _____
private hire /praɪvət haɪə(r)/ _____
rate /reɪt/ _____
return ticket /rɪˈtɜːn ˈtɪkɪt/ _____
scale /skeɪl/ _____
scheduled flight /ˈʃedjuːld flaɪt/ _____
security checks /sɪˈkjʊərɪti tʃeks/ _____
surcharge /ˈsɜːtʃɑːdʒ/ _____
take-off /ˈteɪkɒf/ _____
toll /təʊl/ _____
travel pass /ˈtrævl pɑːs/ _____
twinned towns /twɪnd taʊnz/ _____
weekly /ˈwiːkli/ _____
window seat /ˈwɪndəʊ siːt/ _____

# Accommodation

**1** Where do you usually stay when you go on holiday? Make a list of all the different types of tourist accommodation you can think of.

**2** Read the text and write the names of the types of accommodation under the pictures.

**1** barge

**2**

**3**

**4**

Nowadays, the choice of tourist accommodation to suit your taste, budget and destination is endless. At the high end of the market there are hotels, offering rooms and meals. Motels are similar, except they are for motorists. So they are generally on major roads and always provide parking, but not always meals. B&Bs, or guesthouses, differ from hotels as they are usually small, less expensive, owner-occupied, family-run businesses without staff on call 24/7. Alternatively, holiday villages are popular with families who may be travelling on a budget. They offer a choice of self-catering accommodation from small wooden cabins or chalets to studio apartments to large holiday villas, all in modern resorts with many leisure and recreational services available on site.

Private holiday rental offers a wide variety of accommodation. Then there are timeshares, where several people own accommodation they can use at specific periods each year. To avoid getting bored with the same destination, how about doing a house swap, where people holiday in each others' houses?

Hostels provide a low-cost, self-catering alternative to hotels, and appeal to young travellers, as the shared dormitories make it easy to meet people. Increasingly, universities offer campus accommodation in students' halls of residence during the holidays. This is the type of accommodation you often find on study holidays, but it can also be a cheap and sociable way to take a city break.

If you're looking for an adventure on a budget, campsites are perfect. You can take your own tent, or even stay in a traditional round Mongolian yurt or a tall Native American tepee. For more comfort, there are also caravans and campervans, which enable you to enjoy a holiday on the move. Finally, if you like to combine transport and accommodation, why not try a barge, a long flat boat which travels on rivers and canals, or a yacht if you prefer the sea.

**5**

**6**

**7**

**8**

**3** Read the text again and choose the correct answer.

1 Hotels are accommodation at the
A budget end of the market.    B high end of the market.    C low end of the market.

2 Guesthouses and B&Bs are different from hotels because they are generally run by
A families.    B one person.    C staff 24/7.

3 You can visit a timeshare
A all year round.    B at a specific time each year.    C only in the summer.

4 House swapping helps you to
A avoid boredom.    B avoid cooking.    C make friends.

5 Hostels appeal to
A couples.    B families.    C young people.

6 Campus accommodation is available for tourists to rent during
A the holidays and term time.    B the holidays.    C term time.

7 For comfortable and mobile campsite holidays try
A campervans.    B tents.    C tepees.

8 Which of these isn't a kind of boat?
A Barge    B Yacht    C Yurt

**4** 🎧 7 **Listen to a man checking in at a hotel and complete his hotel registration form.**

## HOTEL INTERCONTINENTAL
### PARIS

(1) Surname: _____
First Name: _____

(2) Address: _____

City: _____ Country: _____ Postal Code: _____

(3) Telephone: _____ mobile: _____
email: _____

(4) Type of room: [delete as appropriate]
☐ single room    ☐ double room **single occupancy**    ☐ double room with bath
☐ shower    ☐ bath & shower

(5) Type of board: ☐ full board    ☐ half board    ☐ B&B

(6) Arrival Date: _____ Departure Date: _____ Total: _____ nights

*I authorise the Paris InterContinental Hotel to charge my credit card with the full amount due.*

(7) Credit Card type: _____ Signature: _____ Room number: _____

**5** Work in pairs. Role play the conversation between the hotel receptionist and the customer and complete the hotel registration form with your partner's information.

**6** Read the text about accommodation services and facilities and complete the table.

> The kind of facilities and services available to you on holiday varies greatly according to your choice of accommodation. Catered accommodation such as hotels, guest houses and B&Bs is generally categorised using a star system which varies from country to country.
>
> Generally one star tends to indicate budget accommodation, offering basic facilities such as en suite bathrooms and TVs in all the rooms and services such as breakfast, drinks and daily room cleaning by chambermaids.
>
> Two stars may additionally offer guests bath towels, complimentary toiletries such as shower gel, a reading light, and a credit card payment facility.
>
> Three star hotels often also provide a hairdryer and telephone in every room as well as internet access either in a public area or in the room, laundry and ironing services, and the hotel reception is staffed for around 14 hours by bilingual staff, speaking English and the native language.
>
> The reception of a four star hotel should be manned for up to 18 hours, have a refrigerated minibar or room service for drinks, and an à la carte restaurant. There would also probably be a lift and more comfortable furniture.
>
> Finally five star luxury accommodation should offer a reception area staffed 24/7 by multilingual staff, a doorman to welcome guests, valet parking, a porter to take luggage to your room, and a safe in the room for valuables. There are often gym and spa facilities available too.

| ★ | ★ ★ | ★ ★ ★ | ★ ★ ★ ★ | ★ ★ ★ ★ ★ |
|---|---|---|---|---|
| en suite bathroom | complimentary toiletries | hairdryer | reception manned for up to 18 hours | reception area manned 24/7 |
| | | | | |

**7** Read the text again and label the pictures with the hotel facilities you see.

**8** Match the hotel staff with the service they provide.

1 chambermaid
2 doorman
3 multilingual staff
4 porter
5 waiter

a ☐ welcoming guests
b ☐ restaurant
c ☐ luggage service
d ☐ reception
e ☐ cleaning rooms

**9** 🎧 8 **Listen to the telephone conversation between a hotel guest and the receptionist. Put a tick (✓) under 'G' for all the services the guest requests, and under 'R' for all the services the hotel receptionist says are available at the hotel.**

| Service | G | R | Specific information about the service |
|---|---|---|---|
| *à la carte* restaurant | | | *Open 12-2 lunchtime and 7-10 for dinner. You need to book a table for dinner.* |
| complimentary toiletries | | | |
| en suite bathroom | | | |
| hairdryer | | | |
| hotel reception staffed 24/7 | | | |
| internet access | | | |
| ironing service | | | |
| laundry service | | | |
| room service | | | |
| safe in the room | | | |

**10** 🎧 8 **Listen again and write specific information about the service.**

**11** **Work in pairs. Role play a conversation between a guest and a receptionist asking and answering about different services. Take notes about the available services, then swap roles. Use these expressions to help you.**

| | |
|---|---|
| Another thing… | I'm calling from/about… |
| Can I help you with anything else? | Is it possible for me to have…? |
| I can't find the… | It/they should be… |
| I'd like to book… for 8 p.m. | There are a few things missing… |
| I'm afraid we don't have… | You need to book… |

**12** **Now write a postcard to a family member or friend telling them about your hotel stay. Use your notes about the facilities and services in exercise 11.**

*Dear _____,*
*I'm staying at the Grand Palace Hotel and the services and facilities are excellent. For example there is…*

## MY GLOSSARY

barge /bɑːdʒ/ _____
bath towel /bɑːθ taʊəl/ _____
cabin /kæbɪn/ _____
campsite /kæmpsaɪt/ _____
chambermaid /tʃeɪmbəmeɪd/ _____
complimentary /kɒmplɪˈmentri/ _____
doorman /dɔːmən/ _____
en suite bathroom /ɒnˈswiːt ˈbɑːθrʊm/ _____
family-run /fæmlirʌn/ _____
guest /gest/ _____
gym and spa /dʒɪm ən spɑː/ _____
house swap /haʊs swɒp/ _____
ironing /aɪənɪŋ/ _____
laundry /lɔːndri/ _____

on call /ɒn kɔːl/ _____
on site /ɒn saɪt/ _____
owner-occupied /əʊnə(r) kjʊpaɪd/ _____
porter /pɔːtə(r)/ _____
safe /seɪf/ _____
single occupancy /sɪŋgl ˈɒkjʊpnsi/ _____
studio apartment /stjuːdiəʊ əˈpɑːtmənt/ _____
tent /tent/ _____
term time /tɜːm taɪm/ _____
timeshare /taɪmʃeə(r)/ _____
toiletries /tɔɪlətriz/ _____
valet parking /væleɪ ˈpɑːkɪŋ/ _____
valuables /væljʊblz/ _____

# 5 | Hotel Staff

**1** Match the following hotel staff positions with their main area of responsibility.

1 Room attendant
2 Concierge
3 Desk clerk
4 General Manager
5 Housekeeper
6 Hotel Porter

a ☐ Takes bookings and checks people in and out.
b ☐ Runs the hotel cleaning.
c ☐ Runs the hotel.
d ☐ Cleans rooms and bathrooms.
e ☐ Carries luggage to and from guests' rooms.
f ☐ Assists guests by arranging tours and making bookings.

**2** Read the text about hotel staff positions and check your answers.

There are many specialist roles in a hotel staff. The **front desk clerk**, often known as the receptionist, takes bookings, checks guests in and out of the hotel, bills them and provides general information. For this role you must be polite, organised and have good language skills.

The **porter**, also called a bellboy, or bellhop in the US, shows you to your room and carries your luggage for you. They may also move and set up equipment for meetings and conferences, take messages and run errands.

The **hotel housekeeper** manages the cleaning staff; supervises their work; draws up their rotas and deals with linen, toiletry and cleaning supplies. They need to be organised, pay attention to detail and have good budgetary skills.

Hotel **room attendants**, more commonly known as chambermaids, make sure hotel rooms are clean, tidy and inviting for guests. They change bed linen and towels; make the beds; vacuum floors; dust and polish furniture; clean bathrooms; replace toiletries and restock the minibar. This role is physically demanding and can often be seasonal or part-time.

The word **concierge** is French for caretaker, but in a hotel they help guests with problems; give them information and assist them with bookings, especially for transportation and sightseeing. A concierge should have good local knowledge and excellent communication skills.

**Hotel managers** oversee all aspects of running a hotel, from housekeeping and general maintenance to budget management and marketing. On a daily basis they manage staff; deal with customer complaints; organise building maintenance and liaise with all the different hotel departments. They need good business and management skills; must be organised and diplomatic; have excellent communication skills and hold hospitality management qualifications.

**3** Read the text again and answer the questions.

Which hotel position...
1 deals with customer complaints? _____
2 is responsible for bookings and bills? _____
3 is responsible for moving and setting up meeting equipment? _____
4 needs good local knowledge? _____
5 orders linen, toiletry and cleaning supplies? _____
6 restocks the minibar? _____

**4** Put the verbs and nouns together to make new phrases.

1 draw up            a ☐ bookings
2 make              b ☐ equipment
3 manage          c ☐ errands
4 run                d ☐ rotas
5 set up            e ☐ staff
6 take              f ☐ the beds

**5** 🎧 9 Listen to different members of hotel staff talking about their jobs. Decide which position each person holds.

Speaker 1 _____      Speaker 4 _____
Speaker 2 _____      Speaker 5 _____
Speaker 3 _____      Speaker 6 _____

**6** Work with a partner and ask and answer questions to find out which role you are most suitable for. Refer back to the text and use these prompts to help you.

| Do you...? | Are you...? | Can you...? | Have you...? |
|---|---|---|---|

A Can you manage budgets?                  A Have you got a hospitality management qualification?
B Yes, I can. / No, I can't really.         B Yes, I have a... / No I haven't.

A Are you diplomatic?                        A Do you understand marketing?
B Yes, I am very diplomatic. / No, I'm not!    B Yes, I do a bit. / No, I don't understand it at all!

**7** Report back to the class what job you think is most suitable for your partner and why.

*I think Xavier should be a concierge because he has a lot of local knowledge and he's...*

**8** Read the four job descriptions and write the correct position in the space.

> Hotel maintenance personnel    Hotel security officer
> Room service attendant    Shuttle/courtesy driver

**1** _____

■ **Job purpose:** serving food and beverages to guests in their rooms, promptly and professionally.

■ **Responsibilities:** taking and delivering orders to guests; clearing trays away from rooms and corridors.

■ **Requirements:** ideally one year working in a restaurant as a server, or other customer service post.

■ **Skills:** interpersonal skills; attention to detail; self-sufficiency; stamina and a good timekeeper.

■ **Career outlook:** an entry-level post, which is generally paid at the minimum national wage; flexible hours and career progression to supervisor or food and beverage manager with training.

**2** _____

**Job purpose:** taking guests between the airport and other destinations, to or around the hotel.

**Responsibilities:** picking up and dropping off guests; loading and unloading guests' luggage.

**Requirements:** experience of different vehicles, roads and driving conditions.

**Skills:** clean driving licence; good road knowledge; good customer service and timekeeper.

**Career outlook:** often a sideways move from other sectors; hours are long but flexible; pay is supplemented by tips.

**3** _____

■ **Job purpose:** ensuring everything in the hotel is working correctly.

■ **Responsibilities:** routine and emergency repairs in hotel grounds, public areas and rooms.

■ **Requirements:** high school diploma and previous experience in similar technical role.

■ **Skills:** self-sufficiency; extensive knowledge of electrics, plumbing, carpentry, health and safety.

■ **Career outlook:** well-paid, technical level post; physically strenuous; no direct career progression.

**4** _____

**Job purpose:** protecting the hotel and its guests against theft, vandalism and trespassers.

**Responsibilities:** patrolling and monitoring hotel and grounds; reporting problems or suspicious events; liaising with the police.

**Requirements:** training provided, but experience of surveillance or law-enforcement preferred.

**Skills:** calm in tense situations; able to take charge in an emergency; self-sufficient and observant.

**Career outlook:** long, unsociable hours; well paid; a sideways move for ex-police or military.

**9** Write the translation of the expressions below in your own language.

1 customer service _____
2 interpersonal skills _____
3 self-sufficiency _____
4 good timekeeper _____
5 entry-level post _____
6 minimum national wage _____
7 clean driving licence _____
8 technical-level post _____
9 physically strenuous _____
10 unsociable hours _____

**10** Choose one of the hotel positions from the opposite page and write a letter of application. In your letter you should:

- indicate which job you are applying for;
- explain what qualifications and experience you have;
- describe your relevant skills;
- explain why you want the job.

Dear Sir/Madam,
I'm writing to apply for...
_____
_____
_____
_____

Yours faithfully,
_____

**11** Complete the job interview between a hotel manager and a room service attendant with the missing information.

> Yes, that's not a problem for me. I prefer working at night.
> That's fine. I want to make a career in the hotel business.
> Thank you very much!
> It's about being polite and making sure guests have everything they need.
> I'm organised and efficient and I work well on my own or as part of a team.
> I'm a server at the Royal Hotel restaurant and I'd like some different hotel experience.

Hotel manager: OK. Tell me why you want the position of room service attendant.
Job candidate: (1) _____
Hotel manager: I see. I suppose you realise that the hours are quite long and antisocial.
Job candidate: (2) _____
Hotel manager: What skills do you think you could bring to this job?
Job candidate: (3) _____
Hotel manager: What do you understand by 'customer care' in a hotel?
Job candidate: (4) _____
Hotel manager: This is an entry-level post so it offers minimum wage with gradual increases.
Job candidate: (5) _____
Hotel manager: I'll have to check your references, but if they are in order, you've got the job!
Job candidate: (6) _____

**12** Work in pairs. Choose a position and role play a job interview. Don't forget to tell the candidate if they got the job or not!

## MY GLOSSARY

budgetary /ˈbʌdʒɪtəri/ _____
carpentry /ˈkɑːpəntri/ _____
chambermaid /ˈtʃeɪmbəmeɪd/ _____
changeover /ˈtʃeɪndʒəʊvə/ _____
complaints /kəmˈpleɪnts/ _____
customer care /ˈkʌstəmə keː/ _____
entry-level post /ˈentriˈlevl pəʊst/ _____
equipment /ɪˈkwɪpmənt/ _____
errands /ˈerənds/ _____
gofer /ˈgəʊfə/ _____
housekeeper /ˈhaʊskiːpə/ _____
law-enforcement /lɔːɛnˈfɔːsmənt/ _____
linen /ˈlɪnɪn/ _____

maintenance /ˈmeɪntənəns/ _____
plumbing /ˈplʌmɪŋ/ _____
porter /ˈpɔːtə/ _____
rotas /ˈrəʊtəs/ _____
shifts /ʃɪfts/ _____
shuttle /ˈʃʌtl/ _____
strenuous /ˈstrenjʊəs/ _____
tip /tɪp/ _____
to liaise /tə lɪˈeɪz/ _____
to patrol /tə pəˈtrəʊl/ _____
to restock /tə riːˈstɒk/ _____
trespasser /ˈtrespəsə(r)/ _____

**1** **What do you need the following for? Talk to a partner.**

| boarding card   driving licence   passport   immunization   visa |
|---|

*I need a boarding card to get onto a plane.*

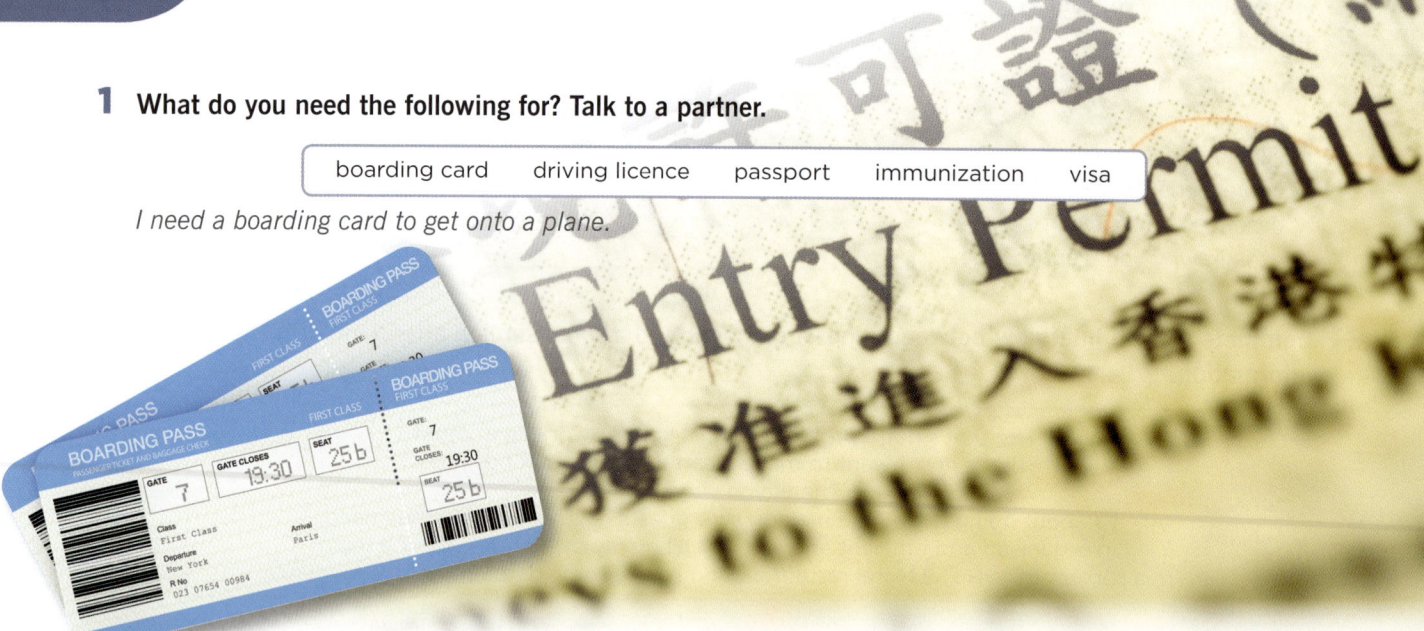

**2** **Read the text about planning and booking a holiday and check your answers.**

Nowadays there are plenty of different ways to book a holiday. Because of advances in technology you can now book holidays over the Internet; by teletext, a system providing news and other information through the TV; over the phone or by going into a travel agency. However you choose to book, you should ensure you have everything you need before departing for your holiday. This might include: valid travel documents such as passports, identity cards or visas for entry into specific countries and maybe your driving licence if you intend to drive your own or hire a car; travel tickets

for planes, ships, trains or coaches and most airlines now expect you to check-in online before you fly and bring your printed boarding card with you to the airport. You should also consider purchasing some form of travel insurance to cover your costs in case your plane is delayed, cancelled, you lose any personal items or there is an emergency whilst you are on holiday. You can buy this independently or directly from your travel agent or travel provider. If you are travelling abroad some banks like you to inform them, otherwise they may block your credit and debit cards when you try to use them overseas. However, it is always wise to take some currency or a pre-paid debit card with you in case there are any problems.

Travel to certain countries requires immunization against diseases. These vary from country to country, as each has different risks to people health-wise, but you should check with your doctor around six weeks before going on your holiday to discuss possible vaccinations you may need for your destination.

**3** **Read the text again and choose the correct answer.**

1 Which of the following are ways of booking a holiday?
   A by phone          B in a travel agency          C over the Internet          D all of these ways

2 Which of the following do you only need for entry into specific countries?
   A identity card          B passport          C visa          D none of these

3 You are expected to check in and print a boarding card before going to…
   A an airport.          B a bus station.          C a ship's port.          D a train station.

4 You might need travel insurance in case you…
   A decide not to travel.          B have an emergency on holiday.
   C lose something before travelling.          D miss your plane.

5 If you don't tell your bank you are going abroad what might they do?
   A Block your cards.          B Close your account.          C Not give you any currency.          D Refuse you credit

6 Some countries require immunization against diseases…
   A when you return from your holiday.          B six weeks before travel.
   C during the holiday.          D before and after the holiday.

**4** 🎧 10 **Listen and complete the travel agent's booking form with the information you hear.**

---

### AURORA TRAVEL AGENCY BOOKING FORM

Type of holiday:
☐ package      ☐ flight only      ☐ accommodation      ☐ other (please specify: _____ )
Destination: _____
Specific dates: _____
Type of accommodation: _____
Transfers: _____

---

**5** **Complete the second part of the conversation with the missing information.**

---

So, I'll need a 50% deposit now and the balance at least 14 days before the holiday date.
So your holiday is a two week, all-inclusive package to the Marmais Resort.      Return flights; transfers to and from
Dalaman Airport; a self-catering apartment, which will be cleaned once a week and use of a communal swimming
pool.      Now your passport numbers and expiry dates.      No problem. You can email them to me.
I also need both your dates of birth.      Can I have the full names of all the people travelling, please?

---

Travel Agent:      (1) _____
Customer:      My name is Karen Miller and my boyfriend's name is Andrew Jones.
Travel Agent:      (2) _____
Customer:      My date of birth is 8 June 1989 and Andrew's is 5 March 1985.
Travel Agent:      (3) _____
Customer:      Oh! I'm afraid I haven't got them with me.
Travel Agent:      (4) _____
Customer:      Ok. Thanks.
Travel Agent:      (5) _____
Customer:      What's included in that?
Travel Agent:      (6) _____
Customer:      Perfect!
Travel Agent:      (7) _____
Customer:      OK. Here's my credit card.

**6** **Work with a partner and take it in turns to role play a travel agent and a customer booking a holiday. Refer back to exercises 4 and 5 to help you.**

Customer:      *I'd like to book a…*
Travel Agent:      *OK…*

**7** **Read the FAQ about the Hotel Excelsior and decide if these statements are true (T) or false (F).**

1  You can't use hotel facilities before checking in or out. ___
2  You have to pay if you want to change your check-in or check-out time. ___
3  Breakfast is at the same time every day of the week. ___
4  It's a good idea to book a table at the restaurant. ___
5  The hotel can change all room bookings. ___
6  It isn't possible to upgrade your room. ___
7  If you cancel more than 48 hours before your stay, you will get all your money back. ___
8  Parking doesn't cost anything. ___

## FAQ

Q: What time is check-in and check-out?
A: Check-in time is 3 p.m. and check-out is 11 a.m.
Q: Can we use the facilities either side of these times?
A: Yes, you can use the facilities before checking in and after checking out of your room.
Q: Are early check-in and late check-out available?
A: Yes, for an additional fee. Please ask at reception.
Q: What time is breakfast served?
A: Breakfast is between 7 a.m.-9.30 a.m. midweek and 8 a.m.-10 a.m. on a weekend.
Q: What time is dinner served?
A: Dinner is served from 7 p.m.-9.30 p.m. every day. We strongly recommend you pre-book.
Q: How do I make changes to my room reservation?
A: If you booked through the hotel, contact us, otherwise contact your travel agent directly.
Q: Can I upgrade my room?
A: If a suitable room is available, you can upgrade your room for an additional fee.
Q: What is your cancellation policy?
A: We require a minimum of 48-hour notice prior to scheduled arrival date for a full refund.
Q: Is there parking available at the hotel?
A: Yes, the hotel offers free valet and self-parking.

*If you have any other questions, please contact reception.*

**8** **Match the words that mean the same.**

1  additional          a ☐ appropriate
2  fee                 b ☐ annulment
3  recommend           c ☐ booking
4  reservation         d ☐ charge
5  upgrade             e ☐ extra
6  suitable            f ☐ improve
7  available           g ☐ obtainable
8  cancellation        h ☐ reimbursement
9  refund              i ☐ suggest

**9** 🎧 11 **Listen and complete the hotel feedback form based on the conversation between a hotel receptionist and the customer checking out.**

## ACORN HOTEL FEEDBACK FORM

Customer name: _____

Room number: _____

Please indicate how much you enjoyed your stay overall:
☐ not at all    ☐ It was OK.    ☐ quite a lot    ☐ very much

Please tell us what you liked about your stay:
_____

Please tell us what you would change or improve about your stay:
_____

Which of the following reflect your check-out experience?
The bill was correct. / incorrect. _____
Staff were helpful. / unhelpful. _____
It was quick and easy. / slow and complicated. _____
Other (please specify). _____

Would you consider a return visit to our hotel?        ☐ yes    ☐ no    ☐ maybe
Would you recommend our hotel to friends or family?    ☐ yes    ☐ no    ☐ maybe

*Thank you very much for your valuable suggestions and comments.*

**10** **Imagine you are Mr Lewis. Write an online review for the Acorn Hotel based on the information in the feedback form. You should:**

- give your review a title, which reflects your overall experience
- describe the good points
- describe the things to improve/change
- say if you would return/recommend the hotel to others
- provide any further useful information

## MY GLOSSARY

amenities /əˈmiːnətiz/ _____
balance /ˈbæləns/ _____
cancellation /kænsəˈleɪʃn/ _____
complimentary /kɒmplɪˈmentri/ _____
currency /ˈkʌrənsi/ _____
discount /ˈdɪskaʊnt/ _____
disease /dɪˈziːz/ _____
expiry /ɪkˈspaɪəri/ _____
fee /fiː/ _____
health wise /helθ waɪz/ _____
immunization /ɪmjunaɪˈzeɪʃn/ _____
inconvenience /ɪnkənˈviːniəns/ _____

insurance /ɪnˈʃʊərəns/ _____
midweek /mɪdˈwiːk/ _____
overseas /əʊvəˈsiːz/ _____
refund /ˈriːfʌnd/ _____
reservation /rezəˈveɪʃn/ _____
resort /rɪˈzɔːt/ _____
risk /rɪsk/ _____
signature /ˈsɪgnətʃə(r)/ _____
to upgrade /tə ʌpˈgreɪd/ _____
transfer /trænsˈfɜː(r)/ _____
vaccination /væksɪˈneɪʃn/ _____
visa /ˈviːzə/ _____

## 1 What do you know about the United Kingdom? Write T (true) or F (false).

1 Great Britain consists of England, Scotland and Northern Ireland.
2 Most of the UK population lives in Scotland.
3 England is agricultural and industrial.
4 The symbol of Wales is a red dragon.
5 Scotland has the same legal, justice, education and banking system as England.
6 Glasgow is the capital of Northern Ireland.

## 2 Read the text and check your answers.

The United Kingdom of Great Britain (England, Wales and Scotland) and Northern Ireland is north-west of mainland Europe.

51 million people live in its biggest country, England, a fertile agricultural region, industrial centre and international melting pot. Cornwall, in the south-west, is perfect for surfers, walkers and art-lovers with its long coastline, futuristic botanical gardens – the Eden Project – and great art galleries. The Norfolk Broads, a canal network in south-east England, offer cycling, boating or bird-watching; and London, the capital, in the south-east, is full of history, style and entertainment.

Wales is a small, mountainous and coastal country with frequent rain from the Irish Sea with an economy based on tourism and agriculture. There are about 3 million people, but 10.2 million sheep! Losing political independence from England in 1282, Wales became semi-autonomous through its National Assembly in 1999, thanks to a strong sense of identity based on language and culture and represented by its symbolic red dragon. Tourist attractions are: the cosmopolitan capital, Cardiff, with its 72,500-seat Millennium Stadium and recently developed Cardiff Bay, with hotels, bars, restaurants, cinemas, museums, an arts centre and a leisure village; Snowdonia and the Brecon Beacons, favourite beauty spots for hikers; and many romantic historical castles.

Scotland is the UK's northernmost country with a harsh climate, dramatic landscapes and a population of just 5.1 million. Scotland was united with England in 1707, but it's very independent due to separate legal, justice, education and banking systems and more recently a devolved parliament. The economy is based on oil and gas, the service sector, and whisky exports. Places to visit include: the beautiful capital, Edinburgh, with an annual arts festival; Glasgow with its Victorian architecture, industrial history and modern music, café and art scenes; the UK's highest mountain, Ben Nevis; its deepest lake, Loch Ness, with its legendary monster; or the wild and remote Outer Hebrides islands with rare wildlife.

Northern Ireland is also semi-autonomous with a population of 1.7 million in the north-eastern part of Ireland. Separated from southern Ireland since the 1920s, it was well-known for the violence between Republicans and Loyalists, which ended in 1998. Its main exports are textiles and machinery. Places to visit include: the capital, Belfast, with its political murals; the Victorian Grand Opera House and the Titanic's Dock; and the breathtaking Giant's Causeway, famous for its incredible rock formation.

**3** Read the text again and complete the factfiles on each country.

**Factfile on England**

Population: _____

Economy: _____

_____

Geography: _____

_____

Capital: _____

**Factfile on Wales**

Population: _____

Economy: _____

_____

Geography: _____

_____

Capital: _____

**Factfile on Scotland**

Population: _____

Economy: _____

_____

Geography: _____

_____

Capital: _____

**Factfile on Northern Ireland**

Population: _____

Economy: _____

_____

Geography: _____

_____

Capital: _____

**4** Read the text again and write these place names on the map of the UK.

> London   Glasgow   Cardiff   Cornwall   Belfast   Edinburgh

**5** 🎧 12   Reorder the conversation below between a tour guide and a tourist. Then listen and check.

| 1 | Tourist: | I'm hiring a car in Scotland this summer. What do you suggest I visit? |
| ☐ | Tour guide: | Yes, it overlooks the sea. It's a really interesting city! |
| ☐ | Tourist: | I hear Scotland has amazing wildlife too. |
| ☐ | Tour guide: | Then you should spend a few days in Edinburgh at the arts festival. |
| ☐ | Tourist: | I want to visit the famous Loch Ness and see the monster. |
| ☐ | Tour guide: | You can visit the castle, which sits on a volcanic rock dominating the city. |
| ☐ | Tourist: | When is that? |
| ☐ | Tour guide: | It's the deepest lake in Scotland and very beautiful, but I can't guarantee you'll see the monster! |
| ☐ | Tourist: | I'm interested in art, history and nature, especially coastlines. |
| ☐ | Tour guide: | Oh yes, especially on the remote islands like the Orkneys. |
| ☐ | Tourist: | Is Edinburgh near the coast? |
| ☐ | Tour guide: | It's on for three weeks in August every year. |
| ☐ | Tourist: | What else can I do in Edinburgh? |
| ☐ | Tour guide: | That depends on what you are interested in. |

**6** Work in pairs. Take it in turns to be the tour guide and the tourist in the following situations. Use the information in the text and the dialogue above to help you.

- You're fascinated by history and legends, especially those with monsters and dragons.
- You have a passion for art, architecture and poetry.
- You're in to hiking, nature and cycling.
- You love city life, going out to restaurants and bars and listening to good music.

**7** 🎧 13 **Listen to this historical sightseeing tour and write the place names under each picture.**

1 _____   2 _____   3 _____   4 _____

**8** 🎧 13 **Listen again and complete the missing numbers.**

Humans first lived in the British Isles about (1) *750,000* years ago, but Britain's most famous prehistoric monument and UNESCO world heritage site, Stonehenge, was probably built in Wiltshire at different times between (2) _____ and (3) _____ BC. The mysterious giant stones set in a unique concentric architectural design are a mixture of nearby sandstone and smaller bluestones from the Preseli Mountains in South Wales, about (4) _____ miles away. We don't know exactly how or why Stonehenge was built, but experts agree it was a ceremonial site for worship and burial and people continue to visit it every year to celebrate the summer solstice.

The Welsh, Irish and Scots originate from the Celts, Indo-European tribes who settled in Britain in about (5) _____ BC and the word probably comes from the Greek *keltoi*, meaning barbarian. The Romans successfully invaded and conquered Britain in (6) _____ BC, establishing the city of *Londinium*, now London, and in the south-west of England, *Aquae Sulis*, Bath Spa, one of the world's finest remaining examples of Roman thermal spas, with natural hot springs of (7) _____ °C.

To keep out the Scots, still regarded as barbarians, the Emperor Hadrian gave order to build Hadrian's Wall from stone and earth, which stretches (8) _____ km from coast to coast across northern Britain.

The Roman rule in Britain ended when the Anglo Saxons from northern Europe began to invade the island in the (9) _____ century AD.

The Vikings from Norway, Sweden and Denmark also invaded Britain in about the (10) _____ century AD, settling in central, northern and eastern England. The modern city of York in the north of England is site of the Jorvik Viking Centre, a settlement where Viking-age houses, workshops and artefacts were excavated.

The Normans conquered Britain with victory at the Battle of Hastings in (11) _____ bringing linguistic, architectural and political changes to Britain. They built mediaeval Motte and Bailey castles, which had raised earth – the 'motte' – under the castle which you could only access across a wooden drawbridge. Around it was a ditch, separating the castle from the 'bailey', that is to say a courtyard surrounded by a wooden fence where servants, tradesmen and craftsmen lived. Windsor Castle, just outside London, the official royal residence for over (12) _____ years, is an excellent example of this kind of castles.

**9** **Read the text and complete the table.**

| Monument | Site | Period | Architectural details | Reason for building it |
|---|---|---|---|---|
| | | *prehistoric* | | |
| *Bath Spa* | | | | |
| | *coast to coast across northern Britain* | | | |
| | | | | *a settlement* |
| | *just outside London* | | | |

**10** 🎧 14 **Match the things to do in London with their descriptions. Then listen and check your answers.**

a The London Eye
b The Tower of London
c The British Museum
d The Globe theatre

e Madam Tussaud's
f Richmond Park
g St Paul's Cathedral
h The Tate Modern

1 [a] Fly above London's skyline for 30 minutes taking in the city landscape for 25 miles in each direction. It's a truly unique experience.

2 ☐ Walk around the largest urban parkland in Europe where you can see over 600 deer, many wild birds, flowers, woods, gardens and ponds.

3 ☐ Explore 900 years of history, see some of the world's largest and most beautiful diamonds in the Crown Jewels, and see the Beefeater guards protecting the tower.

4 ☐ Hang out with the rich and famous at the famous waxworks museum. Visit the Chamber of Horrors to find out the worst of British crime!

5 ☐ Visit one of the world's oldest and finest museums, with one of the biggest world heritage collections from ancient Egypt, Western Asia, Greece, the Orient, Africa and Italy.

6 ☐ Visit the world's most popular contemporary art gallery. The building and its location on the Thames are as interesting as the art inside it.

7 ☐ Experience Shakespeare's theatre as it was meant to be, in an open-air amphitheatre, rebuilt on the Thames river bank.

8 ☐ Possibly London's most famous and iconic church with its impressive architecture and don't miss the magical whispering gallery on the top floor!

**11** **Work in pairs or small groups. Read the short descriptions of things to do and visit in London again and write a short guided tour for a tourist interested in nature, art/culture, history, leisure and theatre. Use these expressions to help you:**

If you want history and culture…
Make the most of your visit and go to…

For theatre enthusiasts, I'd recommend…
Nature lovers shouldn't miss…

## MY GLOSSARY

| | |
|---|---|
| artefact /ɑːtifækt/ _____ | melting pot /meltɪŋ pɒt/ _____ |
| arts festival /ɑːtz ˈfestɪvəl/ _____ | Norman /nɔːmən/ _____ |
| barbarian /bɑːˈbeəriən/ _____ | parkland /pɑːklænd/ _____ |
| Beefeater /ˈbiːfiːtə(r)/ _____ | pond /pɒnd/ _____ |
| burial /ˈberiəl/ _____ | service sector /ˈsɜːvɪs ˈsektə(r)/ _____ |
| cosmopolitan /kɒzməˈpɒlɪtən/ _____ | skyline /ˈskaɪlaɪn/ _____ |
| courtyard /ˈkɔːtjɑːd/ _____ | textile /ˈtekstaɪl/ _____ |
| craftsman /ˈkrɑːftsmən/ _____ | tribe /traɪb/ _____ |
| Crown jewels /kraʊn ˈdʒuːəlz/ _____ | Victorian /vɪkˈtɔːriən/ _____ |
| ditch /dɪtʃ/ _____ | Viking /ˈvaɪkɪŋ/ _____ |
| drawbridge /ˈdrɔːbrɪdʒ/ _____ | waxwork /ˈwækswɜːk/ _____ |
| harsh /hɑːʃ/ _____ | wooden /ˈwʊdən/ _____ |
| loch /lɒk/ _____ | worship /ˈwɜːʃɪp/ _____ |

# 8 International Tourism: Europe

**1** **Do you recognise these tourist destinations in Europe? Match the names with the pictures.**

> Monte Carlo  Lapland
> Ibiza
> Greenland  Algarve

**2** **Read the text and check your answers.**

Europe is extremely varied. Greenland, in the north, is largely in the Arctic Circle with deep fjords, glaciers and icebergs, and summer sees endless days and winter endless nights. Many people take nature and cultural holidays to see wildlife like polar bears, reindeer, and whales and experience the unique Inuit culture.

North-east is Lapland, Finland's northern wilderness providing amazing views of the Northern Lights, Aurora Borealis, a spectacular colourful display of lights caused by solar wind entering the earth's atmosphere. Summer is great for hiking and white water rafting adventures, whilst winter tourism includes snowmobiling, sled safaris, skiing and visits to Santa Claus's Village at Christmas.

Europe also offers sun, sea and sand in its southern Mediterranean countries. Spain's four Balearic Islands have everything for recreational tourism. Ibiza, for example, is the choice for young, trendy, party-going tourists, while Mallorca is a favourite for family beach holidays, but also great for mountain hikes. Menorca is a quieter island, with UNESCO archeological and natural sites. Finally, Formentera, the smallest island, is the destination for tourists who just want to relax.

The Algarve region, on the west coast of Portugal, is well-liked too by beach tourists because of wide sandy beaches, natural bays and breathtaking cliffs.

For the wealthier, more chic tourist, the French Riviera remains fashionable. In Nice, tourists can combine recreation and culture: sunbathing, visiting Impressionist art galleries, eating delicious French cuisine, practising water sports and drinking cocktails.

Along the coast is the small, but nevertheless rich nation of Monaco. It's famous for casinos, its glamorous royal family and the formula one racing track at Monte Carlo, but don't go there unless you're looking for luxury tourism!

**3** **Read the text again and complete the table.**

| Country/Region | Type of tourism | Things to see and do |
|---|---|---|
| Greenland | nature or cultural | fjords, glaciers, icebergs; wildlife like polar bears, reindeer and whales; experience the unique Inuit culture |
| | | |
| | | |
| | | |
| | | |
| | | |

**3**

**4**

**5**

**4** **Read the text again and match the words with their definitions.**

1 Aurora Borealis    a ☐ a journey to watch, take pictures of or hunt wild animals
2 Fjord    b ☐ a very large mass of ice moving slowly
3 Iceberg    c ☐ a thin strip of sea between high rocks typical of Scandinavian countries
4 Glacier    d ☐ a luminous atmospheric display visible in the Northern Hemisphere
5 Safari    e ☐ a large piece of ice moving in the sea with a small amount above the surface of the water

**5** 🎧 15 **Read this conversation between a tour group leader and a travel agent planning a European trip and complete it with the questions below. Then listen and check.**

> ~~Sure. Which period of the year would you like to travel and for how long?~~
> Do you know if there is any chance of seeing the Northern Lights at that time of the year?
> And what kind of things are your group interested in?
> Some of my group have expressed an interest in health tourism too. Is that possible in Greenland?
> What other activities can my group do in Finland?

Group Leader:    Hello, I'm planning to take a tour group over to northern Europe from the UK next year and I'd like you to recommend some itineraries.

Travel Agent:    (1) *Sure. Which period of the year would you like to travel and for how long?*

Group Leader:    Sometime in spring so the weather is not too hot, maybe for about three weeks.

Travel Agent:    (2) _____

Group Leader    Well, it's quite a mixed group in terms of age and interests so I want to include something that will appeal to everyone.

Travel Agent:    I'd certainly recommend Greenland to you because you can see some amazing wildlife and you also get to take boat trips along the fjords.

Group Leader:    (3) _____

Travel Agent:    I would say that Iceland is more suitable because of the geysers and hot springs. There are lots of modern spa resorts you could stay at.

Group Leader:    (4) _____

Travel Agent:    The best time to see them is in winter, but if you go to remote regions like Lapland without artificial lights, it is sometimes possible to see them.

Group Leader:    (5) _____

Travel Agent:    At that time of the year there are great hiking and white water rafting trips which are really good for developing a team spirit.

**6** **Work in pairs. One of you is a travel agent and the other is a tour group leader. Discuss and plan an itinerary for southern Europe. Use the dialogue above and the text in exercise 2 to help you.**

Student A: *Hello, I'm planning to take a group of tourists to southern Europe.*
Student B: *When are you planning to travel?*

**7** **Answer these questions about European culture and history.**

1 Where do most European cultures and civilisations originate?
   A Greece          B Turkey          C Russia

2 Which city is dominated by the Acropolis and the Parthenon rising above it?
   A Athens          B Berlin          C Paris

3 Which of these is one of the Seven Ancient Wonders of the World?
   A The Coliseum     B The Kremlin      C The Temple of Artemis

4 What is the city of Istanbul the gateway between?
   A Africa and Europe  B East and West   C North and South

5 Which country would you visit for a special bath?
   A Greece          B Turkey          C Russia

6 Which country is so vast that it is better explored as separate countries?
   A Bulgaria         B Poland          C Russia

7 What colour is the main square in Moscow?
   A Pink             B Red             C Yellow

8 Which type of architecture can you find in St Petersburg?
   A French           B Greek           C Italian

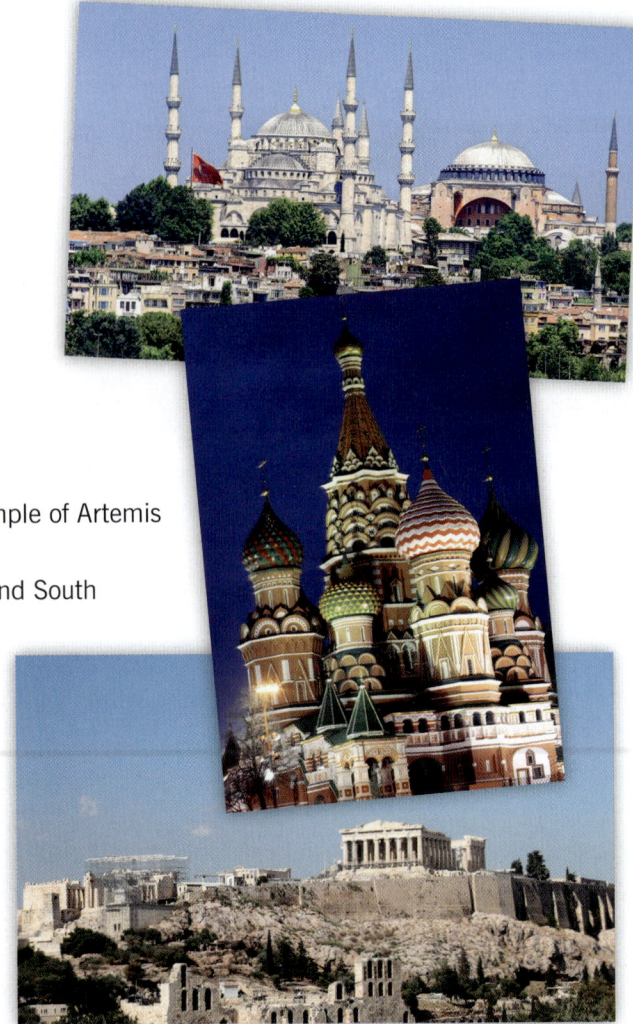

**8** **Read the text and check your answers.**

Europe's history is rich and varied, but most of its culture and civilisations originate in Ancient Greece, from philosophy to democracy to theatre to sport. The modern capital, Athens, provides a real sense of the past, thanks to excavated remains of ancient ruins displayed behind glass in the metro, the Evzones – presidential guards in traditional dress – and the Acropolis World Heritage Site with its iconic white marble Parthenon temple rising above and dominating the city.

Home to one of the Seven Ancient Wonders of the World, the Temple of Artemis at Ephesus, Turkey, is also steeped in centuries of culture and history. Long contested by East and West, thanks to its position as gateway between the two, the capital, Istanbul, has many architectural masterpieces such as the Aya Sofya Muslim Mosque with its beautiful interior, and the emblematic Seven Hill Mosque skyline. You can also enjoy the colourful bazaar district, take a Turkish bath and taste typical meze starters.

Russia is so vast and culturally diverse that it is better explored as separate countries. Its capital, Moscow, is home to cutting-edge music, theatre and art, underground nightclubs and great places to eat. The centre of Moscow unites the Russian history of Tsars, religious Patriarchs and communism in the iconic red-brick Kremlin and nearby Red Square.

The city of St Petersburg, in the north-west, has an impressive network of canals, baroque and neoclassical Italian architecture and is very progressive.

**9** **Read the text again and find the words for the definitions below.**

1 Special presidential guards wearing traditional clothes in Athens: *Evzones*

2 A building used for worship in ancient times and in some religions like Hinduism today: _____

3 A building where Muslims worship: _____

4 The shapes of buildings or mountains against the sky: _____

5 A market typical of the Middle East or South Asia: _____

6 A type of bath where you sit in a very hot, damp room: _____

7 A selection of hot and cold starters in Turkish, Greek or Middle Eastern cuisine: _____

8 The most modern and advanced development in arts or technology: _____

9 The men who ruled Russia before it became a republic: _____

10 A religious leader in the Greek or Russian Orthodox Christian churches: _____

**10** Read the brochure below and write the questions you would like to ask the travel agency.

## THE HISTORY OF BERLIN (12 days)

Don't miss your chance to experience a vibrant culture and visit the places that witnessed some of the most crucial events of the 20th century. Join us on our exciting journey through the history of Berlin!

The itinerary includes:
- The Brandenburg Gate and the Memorial Church, impressive symbols of the city's determination to rebuild during the post-war era;
- the Reichstag, the German parliament building with its glass cupola designed by Sir Norman Foster;
- the Zoological Gardens with one of the world's foremost animal collections;
- a visit to formerly Communist East Berlin;
- a trip to the Checkpoint Charlie Museum where the famous watch tower stood on the border crossing between East and West Berlin.

Other features of our educational trip are:
- a trip to Potsdam, the UNESCO World Cultural Heritage site famous for its magnificent Sanssouci Palace, the Prussian royal summer residence;
- visits to the underground shelters used to protect people during World War II.

Trips can be tailor-made to suit your group's requirements and you will receive a resource pack to prepare your students for their visit. Don't hesitate, contact us now to find out more about dates, cost and accommodation.
info@edutravel.net

**11** You are a teacher and you have just read the brochure above from Edutravel. Write a reply e-mail asking the questions in exercise 10. Include information about:

- your group (name of the school and age of your students)
- the time of year you would like to travel and the length of the trip
- the parts of the itinerary you are interested in

I am writing to request further information about…
I am organising a school trip to…
I wonder if you could tell me…

Could you confirm that…
I look forward to hearing from you…

## MY GLOSSARY

ancient /ˈeɪntʃənt/ _____
to be steeped in (history) /tə bi stiːpd ɪn ˈhɪstəri/ _____
tailor-made /ˈteɪləˈmeɪd/ _____
civilisation /ˌsɪvəlaɪˈzeɪʃən/ _____
cliff /klɪf/ _____
contested /kənˈtestɪd/ _____
cutting-edge /ˈkʌtɪŋˈedʒ/ _____
gateway /ˈɡeɪtweɪ/ _____
glacier /ˈɡlæsɪə(r)/ _____
Greenland /ˈɡriːnlənd/ _____
hot spring /hɒt sprɪŋ/ _____
Inuit /ˈɪnjuɪt/ _____
Lapland /ˈlæplænd/ _____

marble /ˈmɑːbl/ _____
Muslim /ˈmʊzlɪm/ _____
party-going /ˈpɑːti ˈɡəʊɪŋ/ _____
racing track /ˈreɪsɪŋ træk/ _____
reindeer /ˈreɪndɪə(r)/ _____
requirement /rɪˈkwaɪəmənt/ _____
Seven Wonders of the World /ˈsevən ˈwʌndərs ɒv ðə wɜːld/ __
shelter /ˈʃeltə(r)/ _____
sled safari /sled səˈfɑːri/ _____
snowmobiling /ˈsnəʊməbiːlɪŋ/ _____
starter /ˈstɑːtə(r)/ _____
to suit /tə sjuːt/ _____
temple /ˈtempl/ _____

**1** Match the pictures and the names of these well-known USA holiday destinations.

> Niagara Falls   Grand Canyon   Boston   New Orleans

1 _____   2 _____   3 _____   4 _____

**2** Read the text and check your answers.

The United States of America is one of the most culturally and geographically diverse countries in the world. The state of Alaska, to the north-west of Canada, separated from the other 49 states, is vast, remote and wild. You can enjoy whale watching or kayaking adventures there.

The north-eastern states of New England appeal to nature lovers because of the beautiful autumn colours, and to cultural tourists because of cities like Boston which has experimental arts museums, indie rock bands, theatre and film festivals and the famous Harvard University. A little further south, on the border between Canada and New York State, is one of America's most breathtaking natural sights, Niagara Falls.

Also of outstanding beauty are the Rocky Mountains, which stretch almost 5000 km along western America between Canada and New Mexico. They are popular for hiking, fishing, camping, skiing and snowboarding. There is a wide range of wildlife to see, including grizzly bears and mountain lions, especially in the Yellowstone National Park.

In the south-west, in the state of Arizona, the Grand Canyon is the most spectacular canyon in the world. 1,800 m at its deepest, it appears red in colour and is home to many species of wildlife, especially birds of prey.

California is full of contrasts. You can go VIP spotting in Hollywood; skiing in the Sierra Nevada mountains; hiking in Death Valley, the lowest, hottest and driest part of North America; or simply surfing and relaxing along the Big Sur with its dramatic coastline and panoramic views.

New Orleans, in the south-east of the USA, is well-known for jazz and blues music and the annual Mardi Gras Carnival. People love the authentic French Quarter with it mixture of European and Afro Caribbean cultures; the nightclubs of Bourbon Street; the shops and restaurants of Magazine Street and the grand mansions on St Charles Avenue.

Florida, known as the 'Sunshine State', separates the Atlantic Ocean from the Gulf of Mexico on the south-east peninsula of the USA. People come to visit the Everglades National Park, the largest subtropical wilderness in the USA where you can see lots of alligators; Disney World, Orlando; or just to experience the Latin American influence on Miami's beaches and nightlife.

**3** Read the text again and find the words or expressions that correspond to these definitions.

1 A very large brown bear that lives in the mountains of the north-west USA: _____
2 A long deep valley with steep sides made of rock: _____
3 A bird that hunts and eats other animals: _____
4 Someone who has special treatment because they are powerful or famous: _____
5 A carnival celebration with parties and street parades; one of the most famous is in New Orleans: _____
6 A large house, which is often very beautiful: _____

**4** Read the text again and match the activities to the places where people can do them.

1 see beautiful colours in autumn
2 listen to indie rock bands
3 see grizzly bears and mountain lions
4 spot VIPs
5 go surfing
6 celebrate the annual Mardi Gras Carnival
7 see lots of alligators
8 experience Latin American nightlife

a ☑6 New Orleans
b ☐ Hollywood
c ☐ Miami
d ☐ the Everglades National Park
e ☐ New England
f ☐ Boston
g ☐ the Rocky Mountains
h ☐ the Big Sur

**5** 🎧 16 Listen to a conversation between a travel agent and a customer about travel advice to the USA and complete the missing information.

Travel Agent: I just want to go through all the things you need to do before you leave for the USA.
Tourist: Sure, no problem.
Travel Agent: First you have to check your (1) *passport* is valid for at least (2) _____ months after you plan to return home.
Tourist: Yes, it is. Do I have to apply for a (3) _____ too?
Travel Agent: No, you don't. There's a visa waiver programme for all UK or EC passports, but you have to apply through ESTA, Electronic System for Travel Authorisation to the USA, online at least (4) _____ hours before your departure.
Tourist: How long can I stay in the USA with this programme?
Travel Agent: You can stay for up to (5) _____ days.
Tourist: OK. What about security at the airport?
Travel Agent: Security is very tight for all US travel, so you should arrive at the airport at least (6) _____ hours before your departure time.
Tourist: Do I need (7) _____?
Travel Agent: Well, you don't have to be immunised against any diseases, but it's a good idea to get comprehensive travel insurance.
Tourist: Right. How about money?
Travel Agent: The (8) _____ is dollars, but you don't need to take out money in advance because you can use credit cards and cash point machines, which Americans call ATMs.
Tourist: OK. Thanks for all your help and advice.

**6** Read the dialogue again and complete the table below about what you need to and don't need to do when you travel to the USA.

| Need to | Don't need to |
|---|---|
| check your passport is valid for at least six months after you plan to return home | apply for a visa |
| | |
| | |
| | |
| | |
| | |

**7** Work in pairs. Take it in turns to role play a dialogue between a travel agent and a customer. Give advice on what he/she needs/doesn't need to do or bring when travelling to your country. Include the following information:

- airport security
- medical insurance
- visa requirements
- money

**8** **Decide if these statements are true (T) or false (F).**

1 The Empire State Building is in Manhattan.
2 Broadway is the financial heart of New York.
3 The Bronx was once considered the richest and safest borough in New York.
4 The Brooklyn Bridge connects Brooklyn to Queens.
5 There is an amusement park on Coney Island, which you often see in old American films.
6 The borough of Queens hosts the US Open Tennis tournament every year.
7 The smallest borough of New York is an island.
8 The Statue of Liberty was a gift from the UK to the USA.

**9** **Read the text and check your answers.**

New York is the largest and most important American city but it is not the capital of the USA. The smallest of its five boroughs, Manhattan, is where most tourists tend to hang out. The skyline is filled with skyscrapers like the Empire State Building and the names of its neighbourhoods reflect its cultural diversity: Chinatown, Little Italy, Spanish and Black Harlem. It is home to the US's financial heart, Wall Street; to the world famous Metropolitan Museum of Art; to Broadway, the centre of entertainment; to the iconic Times Square and to the fashionistas' favourite street, Fifth Avenue.
The Bronx is New York's most northerly borough and was once considered the poorest and the most dangerous. Today tourists go to visit the New York Yankees' Baseball Stadium, the New York Botanical Garden, the Bronx Zoo, and to see fine examples of Art Deco architecture.
Brooklyn is the most industrialised borough and has the largest population. It is connected to Manhattan via the famous Brooklyn Bridge. It is also home to the Brooklyn Botanic Gardens, Jamaica Bay Wildlife Refuge and the Coney Island amusement park you often see in old American films.
Queens, situated on the east of the city, is the largest borough. It has two airports, JFK and La Guardia and several important film studios. It is also New York's sporting centre, home to the NY Mets baseball team, the US Open annual tennis tournament, and the Aqueduct Racetrack. It is the most ethnically varied borough, which is evident in the restaurants and travel agencies from various nations in the area.
The least populated and most rural borough is Staten Island. It is connected to Manhattan via the Staten Island ferry and to Brooklyn by a bridge. People go hiking or camping there to escape urban life, and there is also a zoo and botanical gardens.
Finally it's difficult to imagine NY without the symbolic Statue of Liberty, a gift of friendship from France to the USA. On Liberty Island in New York's port, it's technically part of the nearby state of New Jersey.

**10** **Read the text again and place the following places on the map of New York.**

> Manhattan   Brooklyn   Staten Island   Liberty Island

**11** **Read the text again and complete the sentences with the correct option.**

1 New York is divided into five *boroughs / neighbourhoods*, the smallest of which is Manhattan.
2 The Empire State Building is the iconic *sporting centre / skyscraper* which attracts millions of visitors.
3 In old American films you can often see the famous Coney Island *amusement park / stadium*.
4 People from different cultures and nationalities live in the different *boroughs / neighbourhoods* of Manhattan.
5 Many Americans enjoy going to the *botanical gardens / racetrack* in the borough of Queens to see horse and dog racing.
6 With its art galleries, huge department stores and international restaurants, Manhattan is the best place to *hang out / go hiking* in New York.

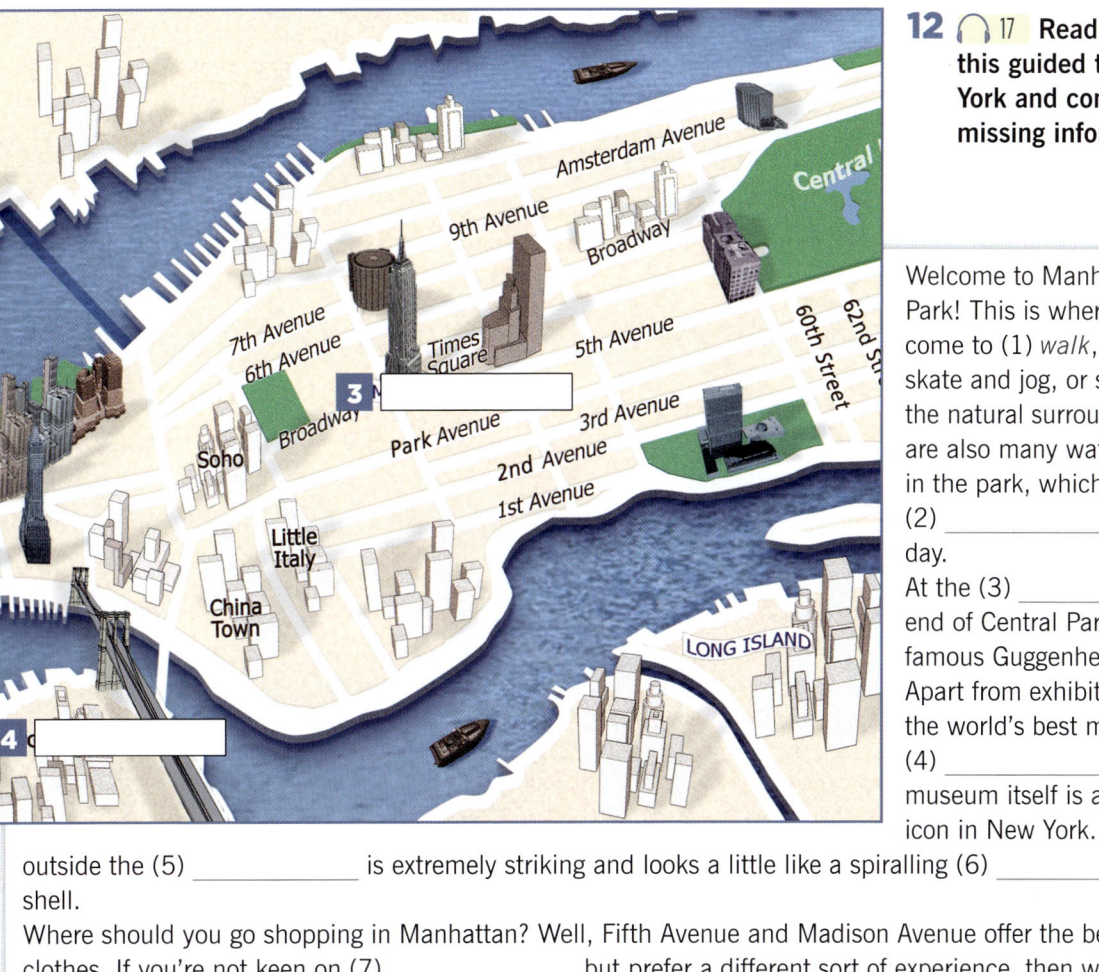

**12** 🎧 17 **Read and listen to this guided tour of New York and complete the missing information.**

Welcome to Manhattan's Central Park! This is where New Yorkers come to (1) *walk*, cycle, line skate and jog, or simply to enjoy the natural surroundings. There are also many water play areas in the park, which are fun and (2) _____ on a hot day.

At the (3) _____ end of Central Park is the famous Guggenheim Museum. Apart from exhibiting some of the world's best modern and (4) _____ art, the museum itself is an architectural icon in New York. From the outside the (5) _____ is extremely striking and looks a little like a spiralling (6) _____ animal shell.

Where should you go shopping in Manhattan? Well, Fifth Avenue and Madison Avenue offer the best in designer clothes. If you're not keen on (7) _____, but prefer a different sort of experience, then why not try Greenwich Village where there are gift shops, (8) _____ and (9) _____ clothes boutiques with reasonable prices.

Finally, you can't visit Manhattan without taking a trip to Broadway, to watch a good show, play or maybe (10) _____ your favourite star!

**13** **Work in pairs or small groups. Research and write a short 'Must Do' guide about one of the places mentioned in the reading text in exercise 9. Use the guided tour above as a model. Include at least one:**

- cultural activity
- nature activity
- leisure/entertainment activity

- other useful or interesting piece of information about the region (time of year to visit, special events, local transport etc.)

## MY GLOSSARY

amusement park /əˈmjuzmənt pɑːk/ _____
ATM (US)/cash point machine (UK) /kæʃ pɔɪnt məˈʃiːn/ _____
bird of prey /bɜːd ɒv preɪ/ _____
borough /ˈbʌrə/ _____
comprehensive travel insurance /kɒmprɪˈhentsɪv ˈtrævəl ɪnʃɔːrəns/ _____
concrete /ˈkɒnkriːt/ _____
cooling /ˈkuːlɪŋ/ _____
department store (US)/shopping centre (UK) /dɪˈpɑːtmənt ˈstɔː(r)/ /ˈʃ pɪŋ ˈsentə(r)/ _____
disease /dɪˈziːz/ _____
gift shop /ɡɪft ʃɒp/ _____

indie /ˈɪndi/ _____
mansion /ˈmæntʃən/ _____
medical insurance /ˈmedɪkəl ɪnˈʃɔːrəns/ _____
neighbourhood /ˈneɪbhʊd/ _____
racetrack /ˈreɪstræk/ _____
shell /ʃel/ _____
steep /stiːp/ _____
striking /ˈstraɪkɪŋ/ _____
sunshine /ˈsʌnʃaɪn/ _____
tournament /ˈtʊənəmənt/ _____
visa /ˈviːzə/ _____
waiver /ˈweɪvə(r)/ _____

# 10 | Ecotourism

**1** Read about ecotourism and match each paragraph with a heading.

> ~~A definition of ecotourism~~   Benefits and Downsides   Organisations involved
> The principles of ecotourism   The future of ecotourism   The history of ecotourism

**1** *A definition of ecotourism*
Any form of tourism – adventure, sports, recreational, cultural or educational – can be based on the principles of sustainable tourism, because it contributes to and doesn't harm the environment it's in. However, ecotourism is a separate branch of tourism altogether, widely defined as: 'responsible travel to natural areas that conserves the environment and improves the well-being of local people'.*

**2** _____
What most ecotourism holidays have in common is their ecological sustainability, their support for local communities, conservation of the environment and of natural resources, their sensitivity towards cultural diversity, and their educational focus.

**3** _____
Ecotourism was developed to meet the needs of the increasing number of nature tourists who were also concerned about the environment. There was an early example of ecotourism in Kenya, East Africa in the 1970s, where people began paying to visit safari parks and the money was used for wildlife conservation. Other successful examples are the nature lodges in the rainforests of Costa Rica and Belize, and recent expeditions to Antarctica.

\* The International Ecotourism Society, 1990.

**4** _____
The greatest danger with ecotourism lies in its popularity. The high number of people means there is a constant need for accommodation, transportation and natural resources, all of which can damage the environment and natural habitats.
On the other hand, Ecotourism also enables us to sustain and support communities and their economies by creating jobs and investing in conservation, development and education projects.

**5** _____
Today many international non-profit organisations are involved in researching and promoting ecotourism. Some of the best known include the World Tourism Organisation, the World Travel and Tourism Council, Tourism Concern and the World Wildlife Fund. Yet ecotourism has become so profitable that there are also many commercial organisations now focusing on this niche market.

**6** _____
Ecotourism is currently the fastest growing market in the tourism industry, but is it too little too late? Have we already destroyed too much of the planet with our environmentally unfriendly mass tourism? In the future will we have to limit the numbers of visitors and increase the cost of travel in order to preserve certain destinations?

**2** Read the text again and try to write a definition for these expressions.

> habitat   ecotourism   niche market   environmentally unfriendly   wildlife conservation   non-profit organizations

**3** Read the text again and decide if these sentences are true (T) or false (F). Correct the false statements.

1 Any form of tourism can be sustainable but that doesn't make it ecotourism. *T*
2 Ecotourism usually has an educational focus.
3 The earliest form of ecotourism was in Belize.
4 The popularity of ecotourism can be a problem.
5 Ecotourism doesn't create jobs.
6 It is possible to make a lot of money from ecotourism.
7 Ecotourism is not a fast growing market in the tourism industry.

**4** Are you a good ecotourist? Take this test and find out!

> **When you're abroad, do you...**
>
> 1 learn words and phrases in the local language and try to use them?
> Yes ☐ No ☐
>
> 2 only visit places that are listed in your guidebook?
> Yes ☐ No ☐
>
> 3 use as much water as you want to wash your hair, body and clothes?
> Yes ☐ No ☐
>
> 4 travel by public transport, hire a bike or walk?
> Yes ☐ No ☐
>
> 5 ask people before taking photographs of them?
> Yes ☐ No ☐
>
> 6 act and dress in the same way as you would at home?
> Yes ☐ No ☐
>
> 7 buy goods produced locally and eat typical local food?
> Yes ☐ No ☐
>
> 8 stay in big luxurious multinational hotels?
> Yes ☐ No ☐

**5** Now match these answers to the quiz. Do you agree with them?

a ☐1 It's a good idea. It shows real respect for the people and culture and is a great icebreaker.
b ☐ It's a good way of supporting local communities and businesses and learning more about a place.
c ☐ Travelling by public transport is a great way to meet local people, and reduce carbon emissions.
d ☐ You should respect people's right to privacy and always ask before taking a photo of a person.
e ☐ Use water carefully. It's a precious natural resource in many countries and Westerners tend to use and waste far more than local people.
f ☐ Keep in mind that many luxurious hotels don't support local economies; they often exploit local people and the environment.
g ☐ Guidebooks are useful for learning about a place before you go, but local people always know the best places to visit. Ask them!
h ☐ Remember that people in different places have different ways of thinking, behaving and dressing and you should respect that. Always ask if you're unsure about taking shoes off or covering your head.

**6** Work in pairs and discuss your answers to the quiz. Use the expressions in the box to help you.

| | |
|---|---|
| To be honest… | Yes, I have / No, I haven't. |
| To tell you the truth… | I've always / never done it. |
| Have you ever… | I've never thought about it before. |

Student A: *When you're abroad, do you learn words and phrases in the local language and try to use them?*
Student B: *Yes, I have always learnt a few words when I've been to another country even if it's only please and thank you.*

**7** Read the texts and match a picture with each one.

A

1 ☐ Have you always wanted to photograph tigers in the wild? Why not take a wildlife photography holiday in India? You'll learn from a professional wildlife photographer and stay in jungle eco-lodges supporting sustainable wildlife parks staffed by locals. Group sizes will be limited to three people.

2 ☐ Have you ever thought about taking a walking holiday in Ireland, combining sea, hills and forests? You'll stay in solar-powered, eco-friendly guesthouses, hiking in small groups, eating locally produced food, learning about Irish culture and nature from your guides and socialising with the locals in traditional Irish pubs.

**8** Read the texts again and complete the table with information in each category.

| Country | Accommodation | Activities | Wildlife and natural habitats | Ecotourism elements |
|---|---|---|---|---|
| India | eco-lodges | photography | tigers | sustainable wildlife parks; group sizes limited to three |
| | | | | |
| | | | | |
| | | | | |
| | | | | |
| | | | | |

**9** 🎧 18 Complete the conversation below between a travel agent and a customer with the expressions from the box. Then listen and check your answers.

conservation projects  eco-resorts  solar-powered  environmentally friendly
natural disasters  raise awareness  renewable energy sources  carbon-neutral

Customer: Hello. I'd like some information about (1) *eco-resorts* in the Maldives. Please.
Travel Agent: Certainly. They are owned and run by native Maldivian staff, who receive fair salaries.
Customer: What about my carbon footprint?
Travel Agent: Well, you might have heard that the Maldives is trying to become the first (2) _____ country in the world and the eco-resorts are contributing to that by using (3) _____ such as wind, water and sun.
Customer: How does that affect the accommodation?
Travel Agent: The luxury chalets are (4) _____ and extremely (5) _____.
Customer: Are there other ways in which the resorts promote sustainability?
Travel Agent: Yes, part of the money you spend on your holiday goes into (6) _____ like cleaning the local coral reef.
Customer: What about cultural and educational projects?
Travel Agent: There are plenty of opportunities to interact with the locals and learn about the wealth of cultural diversity, which makes up these islands. There are also educational projects to (7) _____ of environmental threats to these islands from (8) _____ like tsunamis and hurricanes.

3 ☐ Have you ever imagined trekking the Inca trail to Machu Picchu, kayaking the fjords of Chilean Patagonia and nature-watching on the Galapagos Islands? Local accommodation, hospitality and guides provide opportunities to interact and learn about Latin American people and cultures.

4 ☐ Have you ever wished luxury didn't cost the earth? Well it doesn't have to if you're relaxing in a new eco-resort in the Maldives, destined to be the first carbon-neutral country in the world. Your money will help finance coral cleaning, waste management, water conservation and renewable energy sources.

5 ☐ Have you ever wanted to get up close to a great white shark? Why not join a team of marine biologists in South Africa monitoring the sharks from boats and cages in the sea? You'll spend most of your time working with a small dedicated group of locals, learning about sharks and educating the general public about them.

6 ☐ Have you ever been on a volunteering holiday? Here's your chance! Come to Cambodia and teach sport, music, art or drama to disadvantaged children. You will live with local host families, learn about the culture and take sightseeing trips to beaches, temples and monkey refuges.

**10** You are a travel agent and you have received an email from a customer enquiring about one of the ecotourism holidays in exercise 7. Write a reply including the details below. Use the expressions in the box to help you.

- activities (nature, adventure, culture, etc.)
- accommodation (eco-lodges, locally run guest-houses, host families, etc.)
- the principles of ecotourism on which your holiday is based (group sizes, local staff, local produce, sustainable energy sources, educational focus, transport, etc.)

I am writing in reply to your letter asking for information about...
I would like to let you know that...

As for the...
I hope that you find this helpful...

**MY GLOSSARY**

biologist /baɪˈlədʒɪst/ _____
carbon emission /kɑːbən ɪˈmɪʃən/ _____
carbon footprint /kɑːbən ˈfʊtprɪnt/_____
carbon-neutral /kɑːbən ˈnjuːtrəl/ _____
coral reef /kɒrəl riːf/_____
eco-friendly /iːkəʊfrendli/ _____

educational focus /edjʊˈkeɪʃənəl ˈfəʊkəs/_____
endangered species /ɪnˈdeɪndʒəd ˈspiːʃiz/ _____
renewable energy source /rɪnjuːəbl ˈenədʒi sɔːs/ _____
solar-powered /ˈsəʊlər paʊəd/ _____
sustainability /səˈsteɪnəˈbɪlɪti/ _____

1

2

**1** Do you recognise these new tourist destinations? Match the names with the pictures.

> the Dolomites  Angola  Morocco
> Dubai  Gothenburg

**2** Read the text and check your answers.

Global economic crises, concern for the environment, the threat of violence, as well as social trends, are just some of the things dictating our choice of new tourism destinations.

Angola, in West Africa, also has bitter memories of a 27-year civil war. This may be why Angola's sandy beaches, wildlife parks and Portuguese architecture have remained unspoilt by tourism, and it's now a hot new destination.

Morocco is just a short budget flight away from Europe, but culturally it's a long haul. Fill your senses with the smells, colours and sounds of North Africa: enjoy a hot steam bath in one of Tangier's hammams; take a trip to the ancient city of Marrakesh; and go on a camel ride in the Sahara desert.

Alternatively, why not take a skiing holiday in the totally man-made resort of Dubai in the United Arab Emirates? It has soft artificial snow, ice sculptures, a short ski run and a sledding hill. Great for beginners, but not quite so good for advanced skiers or the environment, as it takes a lot of energy to create a snow world in the heat of the Middle East!

Meanwhile, in Sweden, a more familiar winter destination, the western city of Gothenburg has become popular for beach tourism. It has a beautiful coastline, excellent seafood, and it's much cheaper than the rest of the country, as well as being home to the biggest amusement park in Scandinavia.

If you really care about the environment and want to save money, take a 'staycation', staying at home and visiting local museums, swimming pools and other attractions, rather than travelling abroad.

You could go to Perugia's Umbria Jazz, go climbing and abseiling in the Dolomites or hike in the spectacular scenery of the Majella National Park in the Apennines.

**3** Read the text again and match these words with their definitions.

| | | | |
|---|---|---|---|
| 1 | reflection | a | [1] a careful thought about something |
| 2 | sledding hill | b | ☐ a holiday where you remain at home and visit places in your own country |
| 3 | social trend | c | ☐ something which has not been changed to make it less beautiful or enjoyable |
| 4 | abseiling | d | ☐ a small mountain you ride a snow sledge down |
| 5 | camel ride | e | ☐ a change or development in people's lives and habits |
| 6 | saycation | f | ☐ a place where you can have a steam bath in Islamic countries, usually with separate baths for men and women |
| 7 | unspoilt | g | ☐ an excursion on camel |
| 8 | hammam | h | ☐ to descend a steep slope by a rope secured from above and tied around one's body |

3

4

5

**4** **Read the text again and decide in which destination you can do these things.**

Where can you...

1 admire ice sculptures? *in Dubai*
2 have a steam bath?
3 eat excellent seafood?
4 enjoy unspoilt sandy beaches?
5 go to the beach in a winter destination?

6 hike in spectacular scenery?
7 see Portuguese architecture?
8 ski in a hot country?
9 go abseiling?
10 visit the Sahara Desert?

**5** 🎧 19 **Listen to the radio interview with a travel agent and complete the table with the destinations that are in and out.**

> Argentina Bogotá Guyana New York The Philippines Rio de Janeiro Tasmania
> Thailand The Amazon The Andaman Islands The Maldives Québec

| Destination in 👍 | Destination out 👎 | Reasons for change |
|---|---|---|
| Bogotá | Rio de Janeiro | It's not as crowded, but it's full of trendy (1) *Latin American* nightlife and entertainment. |
| | | It has unique (2) _____ and offers spectacular (3) _____ islands for great diving opportunities. |
| | | People are tired of the over popularity. There are (4) _____, crystal seas and amazing corals and (5) _____. |
| | | It's got a lovely (6) _____, great markets and designer boutiques, as well as (7) _____ and nightlife. |
| | | It has undiscovered tropical (8) _____; rapids and (9) _____ for rafting; a table top mountain for climbing and abseiling. |
| | | For (10)_____, the food is fresh, healthy, tasty and it's definitely different! |

**6** 🎧 19 **Listen again and complete the missing information about the reasons for change.**

**7** Can you name these well-known international sporting events?

1 _____  3 _____  2 _____  4 _____

**8** Read the text and check your answers.

Sports tourism to international sporting events is a growing trend in the tourism industry.

Probably the most popular international sporting events are bicycle races such as the annual Tour de France, which attracts 12 to 15 million spectators along the route. Tourists are mostly domestic, but they still travel many kilometres to watch and support their cycling heroes.

For international travellers the most popular events are the FIFA football World Cup and the Olympics, followed by the European Football Championships. For instance, around 3.18 million fans attended the 2010 FIFA World Cup in South Africa, the first African nation to host the championship, and there are hopes for even more tourists at the 2014 World Cup which will be held in football-crazy Brazil.

Other popular sporting events such as the Rugby Union World Cup and the Cricket World Cup, which both happen every four years, and the Formula 1 Gran Prix also draw a large number of international visitors. The Monaco Grand Prix, alongside the US Indy 500 (Indianapolis 500) and the French Le Mans, is one of the most famous motor racing fixtures of the year, attracting 200,000 visitors in just four days!

So why do people like sports tourism? Surprisingly, the more sport we watch on TV, the more we want to watch live. Sports tourism is much more appealing in general these days, as events offer more comfort and entertainment as well as cheap travel options such as low-cost airlines. The kind of person participating in sports tourism rather depends on the sport they're watching, but statistics show the majority are young, middle-class people aged 18-35. However, rugby and cricket fans tend to be older and wealthier, athletics fans younger and on a tighter budget, while followers of formula 1, usually older, richer and male.

**9** Read the text again and choose the correct answers to complete the sentences.

1 Sports tourism is becoming
  A expensive.      B less popular.      C more popular.

2 Most of the visitors to the Tour de France are
  A foreign.      B French.      C local.

3 In 2010 South Africa was the first African host of
  A the FIFA World Cup.      B the Olympics.      C the Rugby World Cup.

4 Indianapolis, Monaco and Le Mans are all venues for
  A cricket.      B motor racing.      C horse-racing.

5 Sports tourism is more appealing nowadays because events offer more
  A comfort.      B discounts.      C celebrities.

6 Generally athletics fans
  A are older.      B are women.      C don't have a lot of money.

**10** Read the text again and complete the table.

| Sport | Important Competitions | When it takes place | Type of tourists |
|---|---|---|---|
| cricket | | | |
| | | | domestic |
| | | annually | |
| | World Cup | | |
| | | every four years | |

**11** 🎧 20 **Read and listen to the conversation below between a travel agent and a customer and complete it with the missing words.**

Customer: I want to travel to Brazil during the FIFA World Cup.

Travel Agent: OK. There are various World Cup (1) *packages* available or you can go as an independent traveller.

Customer: I'd prefer to be independent because I'm travelling with my girlfriend and she wants to do some (2) _____ and have a bit of a beach holiday too.

Travel Agent: Well, the first thing you need to decide is which games you'd like to (3) _____. We have a list of all the (4) _____ and the possible teams who will be playing there.

Customer: I see. What about travelling around the country?

Travel Agent: It depends a bit on how many games you want to see and where they are located, but you can (5) _____, fly or travel by public transport.

Customer: I'm not sure. What would you advise?

Travel Agent: Once again, it depends on what type of holiday you want. Car hire is quite cheap and you're independent, but traffic is (6) _____ especially in the big cities. Air travel is more expensive, but more relaxing and public transport is fun but it will be extremely (7) _____ during the World Cup.

Customer: I think we'd like to hire a car there. Can we book accommodation through you as well?

Travel Agent: Certainly! I'll (8) _____ some costs and dates and get back to you as soon as possible.

**12** **Work in pairs and take it in turns to role play conversations between a travel agent and a customer who wants to find out more information about the sporting events below. Use the conversation above and the information in exercise 8 to help you.**

- Olympic Games in…
- Tour de France
- Monaco Grand Prix
- Cricket World Cup

Student A: *I'd like to travel to the Monaco Grand Prix.*
Student B: *Are you interested in a package holiday or do you want to be an independent traveller?*

**13** **You are a travel agent and you have received the email below from head office asking you to briefly describe five new travel destinations/activities for people in Italy. Work in small groups and plan and write a reply.**

---

Send   Chat   Attach   Address   Fonts   Colors   Save As Draft

Subject: 5 new holiday destinations

Dear Colleagues,
As competition increases from DIY online holiday bookings, we are asking all our travel agents to come up with some new holiday destinations and activities in each area. We would like you to make a short list of five: one sports based; one staycation idea; one cultural holiday; one recreational holiday; and one other of your choice. Please write a brief paragraph describing each one and email it to me ASAP.

Best wishes,
Tony Good
European Manager
Dream Travel

---

*Dear Mr Good,*
*In response to your email here are our 5 new holiday destinations for…*

## MY GLOSSARY

abseiling /ˈæbseɪlɪŋ/ _____

ASAP (As Soon As Possible) /əz suːn əz ˈpɒsəbl/ _____

to come up with /tə cʌm ʌp wɪð/ _____

to dictate /tə dɪkˈteɪt/ _____

to draw /tə drɔː/ _____

fixture /ˈfɪkstʃə(r)/ _____

follower /ˈfɒləʊə(r)/ _____

football-crazy /ˈfʊtbɔːl ˈkreɪzi/ _____

ice sculpture /aɪs ˈskʌlptʃə(r)/ _____

middle-class /mɪdl klɑːs/ _____

motor-racing /ˈməʊtə(r) ˈreɪsɪŋ/ _____

ski run /skiː rʌn/ _____

sledding hill /ˈsledɪŋ hɪl/ _____

spectator /spekˈteɪtə(r)/ _____

tasty /ˈteɪsti/ _____

unspoilt /ʌnˈspɔɪld/ _____

**Flash on English for Tourism**

*Editorial coordination:* Simona Franzoni
*Editorial department:* Pauline Carr, Serena Polverino
*Art Director:* Marco Mercatali
*Page design:* Sergio Elisei
*Picture Editor:* Giorgia D'Angelo
*Production Manager:* Francesco Capitano
*Page layout:* Sara Blasigh

**Cover**
*Cover design:* Paola Lorenzetti
*Photo:* Shutterstock
© 2012 ELI S.r.l
P.O. Box 6
62019 Recanati
Italy
Tel. +39 071 750701
Fax. +39 071 977851
info@elionline.com
www.elionline.com

Printed by Tecnostampa - Pigini Group Printing Division, Loreto - Trevi     12.83.274.0

ISBN 978-88-536-1447-6

**Acknowledgements**
ELI Archives: pp. 16 (photo 3, 4, 6), 18;
Laura Bresciani: pp. 38-39;
Shutterstock: pp. 3, 4, 5, 6, 7, 9, 10, 11, 12, 13, 16 (photo 1, 2, 5, 7, 8), 17, 20, 21, 22, 24, 25, 26, 28, 29, 30, 31, 32, 33, 34, 35, 36, 37, 40, 41, 42, 43, 44, 45, 46.